"Pass!" [...]
The Panther [...] [str]eaks backward, and sure enough, Raghib "Rocket" Ismail is slanting up the middle, right at Chad. Chad steps back, but Rocket keeps coming at full speed. He's using the umpire as a pick! The plan is to run the defender at Chad, then streak by and catch the quick pass up the middle.

The thing is, Chad *owns* the meat grinder and doesn't want Rocket or anyone else in *his* house. As Rocket blows by, Chad lowers his shoulder and levels him. Rocket hurtles backward as if he's been shot. He flops into the soggy turf. Shaken, Rocket scrambles to locate who nailed him, expecting to see Ken Norton. But the only one around is the umpire . . .

Inside The Meat Grinder

CHAD BROWN
and Alan Eisenstock

St. Martin's Paperbacks

INSIDE THE MEAT GRINDER

Copyright © 1999 by Chad Brown and Alan Eisenstock.
Cover photograph © Paul Spinelli/NFL Photos.

Library of Congress Catalog Card Number: 99-35780

ISBN: 0-312-97653-4

Printed in the United States of America

St. Martin's Press hardcover edition / September 1999
St. Martin's Paperbacks edition / September 2000

10 9 8 7 6 5 4 3 2 1

CHAD:

for my mom, Everdee Battee

ALAN:

for Bobbie, Jonah, Kiva, and, forever, Zachary

CONTENTS

ACKNOWLEDGMENTS

There are many people who helped make this book possible. We are especially grateful to:

Aaron Priest, the Sam Huff of literary agents who said, "For chrissakes, put me on the *field*," or words to that effect. You were right. You're always right.

Lisa Vance, Aaron's intrepid right hand, who took every frantic and stupid question with patience and grace.

Joe Veltre, a perfect editor, who managed always to nudge ever so gently and edit ever so judiciously, although I did go to sleep some nights to the sound of your voice shouting in my head, "Where are those *photos*?"

Jim Arehart of *Referee Magazine,* the matchmaker who put Chad and me together, initially for an article I wrote, "Standing Tall," which appeared in the September '98 issue. The result was a deep and valued friendship with Chad, and this book.

Ed Hochuli and Jerry Markbreit, two of the best NFL referees ever, who also served as legal counsel, sounding boards, and voices of reason and support.

Red Cashion, living legend, an inspiration to anyone who even *thinks* about wearing stripes; and Chuck Stewart, partner at Personal Touch, thanks for your time and participation in the Round Table.

John Carlos, thanks for keeping the facts straight about Commerce, especially about the Great Car Adventure; and Dion Veloz, thanks for the use of your desk and for the great job you do every day.

For Chad: Deborah Brown, life partner and best friend. Your intelligence, strength, support, and spirit have always sustained me. Thank you for going over the book with a fine-tooth comb. Trent and Devin, I love you; you both give me such joy. If you want to get into the family business, officiating in the NFL, you have my blessing.

For Alan: My group of incredible friends and family who gave me constant encouragement and good cheer, a laptop, and more than one lift home; Kathy Montgomery, Jeff Chester, Susan Alon, Susan Baskin, Richard Gerwitz, Sue Pomerantz, George Weinberger, Alison Ritz, Jessica Ritz, and especially, my parents, Jim and Shirley Eisenstock; Randy Feldman—our daily phone calls kept me sane; Larry Mintz—you have been the best friend and partner anyone could have; and Madeline and Phil Schwarzman—you have taken care of the kids, Lefty, and me more than you will ever know. I cannot express enough my thanks and love to you all.

To David Ritz, role model, dearest friend, you've believed in me longer and more passionately than I have believed in myself. Thank you is not enough, but it'll have to do.

Special thanks to the three most extraordinary people I have ever met: Jonah and Kiva, super readers, and the best children and friends I could ever have. You make me smile every minute of every day.

And my wife Bobbie. I could not have written this book without you. Your keen eye and remarkable insight guided me through every page. I appreciate you always, whether you are standing beside me or over me. And, you can do more with one hand than most people could do with three. Thank you forever.

COIN TOSS

The Super Bowl.

The biggest single event in sports.

And I'm here, thought Chad Brown. *Invited. Chosen, in fact, by the National Football League. Hell, one of the chosen few. One of only nine officials selected out of the whole league. One out of 113.*

Well, I deserve it. Chad nodded to himself. *I worked my butt off, and despite all the crap that happened this year—the flubbed coin toss in Detroit, the blown Hail Mary call in New England, the phantom touchdown call in New York when Testaverde missed the goal line by a good foot, fans and coaches screaming first for our heads, then for instant replay, and officials on the front page of the* New York Times—*I had a helluva year. The key was staying within myself,* Chad reasoned. *Trying not to cover the whole field, trying not to do too much, not looking to make the call that nobody else saw. And it worked out. Here I am.*

An alternate to the Super Bowl.

OK, true, I'm not actually going to work the game. Unless Jim Daopoulos, the umpire, or one of the other officials suddenly comes down with food poisoning or a smashed toe or something and can't answer the bell. Happened last year. The umpire got hurt and the alternate got in. Of course, I'm not wishing that on anybody. It's an honor just being named an alternate. I'm sure I missed being selected to the crew by a hair. It's like being voted the first runner-up to Miss America. Lot of responsibility. If Daopoulos can't assume the duties of Miss America, then I jump in, to save the day. Damn. The Super Bowl's a piece of cake. It's the easiest game of the year to officiate. You have the two best teams, usually the two most mistake-free teams, and the game is almost always a blowout. Man, I'd love to work this game.

It's my dream, thought Chad. *It used to be my goal. Then it became my passion, then my mission. Being named an alternate this year is just motivating me to be named to next year's crew. Damn. I'm daydreaming. Gotta get back to my job. Super Bowl's starting in an hour and I've got to finish up here. Talk about responsibility. I may be an alternate and I may not be officiating the Big Dance, but what I'm doing here is critical to the game itself. In fact, if I don't pull this off, don't do it exactly right, the Broncos and the Falcons don't play this game. Talk about a pressure job. Nothing but pressure. Hell, a job like this can really pump you up. . . .*

"Chad, those balls pumped up yet?" Bernie Kukar, the referee for the Super Bowl, pokes his head into the equipment room and breaks Chad Brown's reverie.

"Oh. Yeah, Bernie. They're all set. Right pressure, too."

"Wiped and counted?"

"Wiped and counted. All sixty-four. Why do we need sixty-four footballs anyway?"

"It's the Super Bowl, Chad. A ball's gonna be given away after every snap in the first quarter."

"No wonder the game takes seven hours. Man, I haven't done this since I was a rookie."

"You haven't lost your touch, Chad," says Kukar, massaging the leather of one of the balls.

"Oh," says Chad. He hands Kukar a small white card the size of an index card. "The Falcons' cast list."

Kukar takes the card from Chad and scans it. It's the rundown of every Atlanta Falcon who's wearing a cast. Another responsibility of the alternates. Studying the card, Kukar wonders, "You see Reeves?"

"Yeah." Chad smiles.

Earlier, Chad had walked along the sideline of Joe Robbie Stadium, squinting into the sunlight, pushing through some nasty humidity, sticky weather for a football game. But as he turned to walk away, he heard Dan Reeves, coach of the Atlanta Falcons, shout toward him.

"Look who we got! Chad Brown. Gonna be awright now."

Chad grinned. He turned to face Coach Reeves, who was approaching with his offensive line coach, Art Shell, a friend of Chad's since his head coaching days with the Los Angeles Raiders. Chad stuck out his hand.

"Congratulations, Coach."

"Thanks, Chad. Couldn't have done it without you."

Through a laugh, Chad offers, "Yeah. I had a lot to do with you being here." Then, sincerely, "Good luck today."

"Gonna need it," and Reeves heads into his locker room. Chad stands a moment with Shell, shooting the shit, talking about the Falcons' amazing 30–27 overtime win over Minnesota in the NFC championship game. No mention of Reeves's recent quadruple bypass. It would be inappropriate. In Chad's mind, two armies are about to go to war. No need to bring up anything negative. Bad form, bad luck. Art Shell grips Chad's hand in an earnest handshake, turns to join his coach.

Chad sighs. Sunday already. He and his wife, Deborah, had arrived on the red-eye early Thursday morning. The four days since were a blur, a whirlwind of banquets and buffets, press conferences, photo ops, game films, a formal dinner-dance, all punctuated yesterday by perhaps the most surreal event of his professional life.

It occurred at midfield, during the *rehearsal* of the coin toss.

Which, by definition, was surreal enough.

It's annoying enough to rehearse the coin toss. To be

fair, there was the coin flip flap this year in Detroit. Lions against the Steelers. Overtime. Standing at the fifty-yard line flanked by the teams' captains, Phil Luckett, the referee, prepares to flip the coin to determine who will get the ball first in the overtime period. He tells Jerome Bettis to call it in the air. Bettis shouts, "Tails!" The coin lands on tails. Luckett says, "You said *heads*. Lions' ball." Bettis goes nuts. He starts jumping in the air like a kid on a trampoline. Months later, Luckett would explain in *Referee Magazine* that he heard Bettis first say, softly, "Heads," then, "Tails," when the coin was in the air. The National Football League trains officials to go with the first thing they hear, so Luckett went with "Heads." The audio track on videotapes of the game bears this out; you can hear Bettis say faintly, "Heads," then, louder, "Tails." At the time, none of this was explained. The subsequent silence resulted in an uproar, the media screaming for the hides of all NFL officials and calling for Luckett's head on a plate. So, maybe a rehearsal of the coin flip at the Super Bowl wasn't such a horrible idea.

In truth, the rehearsal is for the TV people. This will not be your ordinary coin toss. In addition to the captains from the Falcons and Broncos and the nine NFL officials, there will be ten members of the 1958 Baltimore Colts and New York Giants who played in what most football historians consider the greatest game ever, the NFL championship game, won in overtime by the Colts, 23–17.

Chad fidgets as an assistant director from FOX-TV tries to camera-block the mob at the fifty. Behind him, standing on a podium, wearing jeans and a high-cut blouse, her provocative image hung on a hanger somewhere, Cher belts out our national anthem to her own prerecorded voice. It's true. The anthem is not sung live. It is lip-synched to safeguard the designated celebrity singer from forgetting the lyrics or going off the deep end musically. The assistant director moves a Colt forward, gently nudges a Giant to fill the gap next to him. It's all about positioning the players to stay on their camera marks, staging the coin toss very specifically so it looks completely spontaneous. This spontaneity, ultimately, will take seven rehearsals.

Chad sighs, decides to focus on who's who.

Former great defensive ends, the two Italian Stallions, Andy Robustelli of the Giants and Gino Marchetti of the Colts, bookend massive Jim Parker, the great Colt offensive tackle. Chad recognizes Art Donovan, former Colt defensive tackle from TV where he is a frequent wisecracking guest on *Letterman*. He spots Frank Gifford, always a bit aloof, standing off to the side. There's Tom Landry, still stiff as a board with a personality to match, known mainly as the coach who turned the Dallas Cowboys around and led them to two Super Bowls. In 1958, he was a member of the Giants' coaching staff. Roosevelt Brown, the powerful ex-Giants' offensive tackle, the best small lineman Chad has ever seen, walks slowly and painfully on reconstructed plastic knees. Chad nods to Lenny "Spats" Moore, legendary Colts running back and wideout, nicknamed Spats because he was the first player to tape his socks *over* his shoes. Raymond Berry, the Technician, the man who ran the most precise pass patterns in history, jokes with Moore and Donovan.

And then Chad becomes aware of a *presence*.

A man he hadn't noticed before.

Chad stares at him for a moment to be sure. He'd heard the man might be here but had dismissed the thought, thinking he'd be too nervous to meet him and wanting to avoid disappointment if he didn't show.

He was here all right. Ten feet away. Joking with his former Giants' teammates. Looking as trim and tough as he did when he terrorized running backs and practically cracked wide receivers in half when they ventured across the middle.

Chad's idol. The man whose number he took in college because he admired him so much. Number 70. The man whom some people called the Assassin before Jack Tatum confiscated the nickname. One of the greatest linebackers ever to play the game.

Sam Huff.

Cher howled, ". . . the rockets red glare, the bombs bursting in airrrr . . . ," and Chad crossed the ten yards to Huff. A thousand questions raced through his mind, beginning with, *Do I call him Mr. Huff? Sam?*, and then Chad was facing him.

"Sam Huff," he blurted out.

"Yes?" A trace of southern drawl dunked in politeness.

Chad cleared his throat and drew his entire six-foot, five-inch frame into attention.

"I'm Chad Brown."

Hand out. Gripped. A boyish smile. Then . . .

"You were my idol growing up. Matter of fact, I was such a fan, I took your number when I was in college."

Another smile. So serene here in street clothes, senior citizen Colts and Giants surrounding him, a young assistant TV director, bursting through his nylon warm-up suit, shouting into a headset, requesting yet another rehearsal, number five, for the damn *coin toss*, and Chad just wants to talk to Sam Huff. Images of Number 70 standing two players straight up who are trying to block him, then crunching some miserable flanker into the ground, dance into his head.

"Jim Brown," says Chad. "Those duels you had. The two of you. Like a heavyweight fight."

"Yeah," says Huff. "He was the greatest runner ever.

So tough to tackle. You couldn't really tackle him alone. Had to just hang on, wait for help."

Chad relaxes, settles in. A million more questions. *I could talk to him forever*, he thinks.

But the assistant director arrives, rearranging bodies like furniture, and steers Sam Huff away.

The moment is gone. But the reason for it reveals itself to Chad. *It's why I'm here, alternate or not, why I played professional football, why I became an official, and why I have to come back here next year, to work the Show.*

I want to become the Sam Huff of umpires.

The best who's ever played the position.

Used to watch him on TV, remembers Chad. *He seemed so unreal, so much bigger than life, so far away.*

And I just shook his hand.

Behind him, Cher reaches for the stars and wails, "The land of the freee and the hommme of the bravve."

Damn. I've come a long way.

FIRST QUARTER
II

1
ROCKET MAN

. . . that was the *worst* officiating I've ever seen. There were so many non-calls. The league has to do something. It's about time they stopped having old men trying to chase around the best athletes on the planet.

—Ray Bentley, former NFL linebacker, current FOX-TV football analyst, appearing on "One-on-One" Sports Talk Radio with John Renshaw (The Freak), Tuesday, November 3, 1998, 8:47 A.M.

Sunday, November 8, 1998. Chad Brown, fifty, NFL umpire, leans in to watch the first play of the Carolina–San Francisco game from his position behind the 49ers' defensive line. He is staked out in the area known as the "meat grinder." It is called the meat grinder because if you didn't have a good sense of the game or fast feet, you were in danger of being chopped up like a slab of hamburger. It had already happened to two umpires this year. Rex Stuart got blindsided by a rampaging lineman in a preseason game and tore up his knee. End of his career. And Bob Boylston, a friend, was trampled by a 320-pound pulling guard who was blocking for the Raiders' Napoleon Kaufman. His hip was shattered. End of his season, and probably the end of his career as well.

Unlike most umpires, Chad Brown was intimate with the meat grinder. He'd lived there for eight years when he played professional football, most of those years in the National Football League. Out of the 113 NFL officials, Chad was one of only three former NFL players. Not only did he know the territory; he knew most of the tricks of the trade:

In the beginning, of course, there was the "Head Slap," immortalized by David "Deacon" Jones. Fairly self-explanatory. Imitating Moe Howard of the Three Stooges, the pass rusher simply whacks the guy blocking him continuously across the side of his helmet (the technical term is *upside* the head) until the poor defenseless offensive player sinks to his knees, holding his head, howling in pain. The slap, after causing perpetual ringing of the ears and several broken eardrums, was, mercifully, banned.

The quickest trick is "the Hump," Reggie White's specialty. This starts with a fake to the inside, followed by either a pivot with a hook, a three-sixty with a hook, or a nearly unstoppable outside whip move with a hook. The Hump may or may not involve illegal use of the hands. The offensive lineman is usually facedown on the ground and Reggie is usually facedown on the quarterback before the official can tell.

Then there is the "Bull Rush," popularized by William "The Refrigerator" Perry. This is a patented headdown, straight-ahead rhinolike charge that made maximum use of Fridge's enormous girth and regularly left the unsuspecting and helpless lineman lying in a divot. The Bull Rush isn't illegal; it's just unfair.

When Perry employed the move, Chad would shake his head and point to the Fridge's stomach, which seemed to hover an inch above his feet. Perry was, by far, the biggest man he'd ever seen play football. "Fridge, I know you're over four hundred pounds. You gotta be."

"I don't know." Fridge shrugged. "They ain't built a scale yet to weigh me."

The most notorious deception of all is "the Rip." This is a sinister move developed by and elevated to the level of low art by Howie Long, the former All-Pro Raiders' defensive lineman, currently a movie bad guy in such films as *Broken Arrow* with John Travolta and a member of the FOX-TV NFL Sunday broadcasting cast of characters. In the Rip, Long would attack the offensive lineman blocking him, shove his forearm up, beneath his opponent's arms, toward his face guard, lock himself there, then ram into the lineman with his shoulder. Two things would then happen: either (1) the lineman would topple over like a felled tree, clearing a path for Long to clobber the quarterback, or (2) the lineman would hold his ground, giving the appearance to the untrained eye that he was holding Long. This was, of course, an optical illusion. Long was holding *him*. The Rip, like any good trick, needed a strong finish. Long had this wired, a clear foreshadowing of his acting career.

"He's holding me!" he'd scream at the officials. "Look! He's holding me! Get over here, for crissakes!"

The first time Chad caught Howie Long in mid-Rip, he immediately tossed his flag.

"Whataya got?" Jerry Markbreit, the referee, jogged over to Chad, his rookie umpire.

"Sixty-seven on a hold," Chad said, pointing to the lineman Howie Long had just Ripped to shreds.

"*What?*" the lineman yelled. "Sonofabitch was holding *me!*"

"Yeah, right," Long said, catching Chad's eye and shaking his head in pity. "You believe it, Chad? These guards'll hold me right in front of you, then *lie* about it."

As Markbreit marched off the fifteen-yard penalty, Howie Long patted Chad gently on the back and added his final, crowning touch.

"Good call, Chad."

Later that week, Chad got a phone call from Jerry Seeman, NFL director of officiating. He told Chad to study carefully the weekly training tape he'd put together. The tape was a compilation of good calls, bad calls, controversial and questionable calls that had occurred during the week. In it, Chad's holding call on Howie Long's Rip move was featured. Seeman stopped the action and, in the manner of John Madden analyzing a play during a game, drew a chalk circle around Long and the lineman, and, to add insult to injury, drew another chalk circle around Chad dropping his yellow handkerchief.

"This is not a hold," Seeman's voice-over announced. "This is a Rip move. The umpire has been duped. In the future, ignore this kind of thing." Chad was never fooled by Howie Long or the Rip again.

Right now, before the first snap of the Carolina–49ers game, Chad is having a hard time focusing. He just can't swat away the memory of a vicious comment he'd heard on the radio trashing the officials for being, essentially, incompetent, out-of-shape old men. The irony is he'd heard the comment during his daily three-mile run. Pissed, he'd switched to another station, only to hear someone on the Jim Rome show say that the officiating this year was officious and they should all be fired. To make things even worse, certain former players turned broadcasters, among them Joe Theismann and Terry Bradshaw, were saying the same thing on their respective pregame forums prior to their Sunday games.

Piling on the officials is not exactly news. Chad remembers a couple of incidents during his rookie season that terrified him. He was convinced then that he would be run out of the league on a rail. *Damn. I thought I'd buried those feelings forever, but here they are, rushing back, knocking me for a loop. I'm about to officiate a ball game. Who needs this crap?*

Hating and baiting the officials are part of the game, necessary evils in a way, but in the beginning Chad couldn't separate the mind game from his own officiating ability. In fact, he was sure everything was personal. He was certain it was all about him. He would come to realize over the years that there was a mental aspect to the game of football, a con game practiced by astute coaches and cunning players like Howie Long, who were always looking for an edge. Having the stripes on your side was a damn good start.

In his first year as an NFL umpire, prior to every game Chad shot out of the tunnel like a cannon. He wanted to cover the entire field like a tarp, see every play, flag every infraction. The meat grinder is a box, consisting of, on offense, the two guards and center and, on defense, the noseguard and tackles. These men were Chad's main responsibility. But in that first season, he not only wanted to patrol *them,* he wanted to patrol everybody: the tight end, running backs, quarterbacks, linebackers, *everybody*. He didn't just want to make calls. He wanted to make *great* calls, calls that were obvious to him but invisible to everybody else.

"Now here is a call the whole officiating crew missed," he wanted Jerry Seeman to say during the next training tape, "except for rookie umpire Chad Brown, who somehow managed to see it, despite the war going on in the meat grinder. Great call, Chad."

That, of course, didn't happen. Not during his rookie season at least. What did happen was that Chad saw calls that weren't there and missed calls that were. Flags flew when they shouldn't and stayed in his belt when they should. In other words, it was a tough, but typical, rookie year.

He remembered being pushed to the brink once that season.

Houston against Buffalo, 1992. Chris Dishman, a Houston defensive back, after being on the wrong end of a late hit and not having a flag thrown his way, leaped to his feet and rushed over to Chad, roaring, "You are a blind sonofabitch!" Chad had had a rough afternoon. There were penalties all day long, and by this point everybody on the field was pretty much on edge. Even Chad was approaching his boiling point.

"What'd you call me?"

"You heard me!"

"Say it again!"

Dishman did, gladly.

Chad shot his flag into the air like he was launching a rocket. Not waiting for it to flutter to the turf, he called Dishman for a fifteen-yard personal foul.

"One more, once, and you are out of the game."

Unlike in baseball, where umpires routinely toss players out of games, football players are rarely run. Dishman took a moment to compose himself and looked into Chad's eyes. Whoa. This guy wasn't kidding. Dishman raised both hands in a somewhat supplicant shrug. The rookie umpire was thrown. He didn't know what to say, so he merely mumbled, "Yeahhh," under his breath and walked away, leaving Dishman standing fifteen yards farther away, the roar of boos cascading down around him like rain.

Also that year, there was the Buddy Ryan incident in the Arizona desert. The Cardinals were locked in a defensive struggle with the New York Giants. No surprise. The Giants had no offense, and Buddy Ryan, coach of the Cardinals, was the architect of the famed Chicago

Bears defense that throttled the New England Patriots 46–10 in Super Bowl XX. As the first half neared its end, Ryan, who'd been ranting and raving along the sideline all game, walked stride by stride with Markbreit, the referee.

"I want to talk to you, Jerry!" Ryan hollered.

Jerry waved an acknowledgment. Then he turned to Chad. "Stay close, Chad," he said.

The gun sounded, ending the half. Chad and Jerry approached Ryan, who was waiting for them at the fifty, hands on hips.

Ryan is a fireplug of a man whose face is etched in a constant scowl. His physical appearance intimidates you, until he speaks. He has a high-pitched voice that squeaks when he raises it in anger. By the time Chad and Markbreit reached him, Ryan had calmed down. He looked them over for a moment, nodded, and spoke.

"We got three teams out there today," he said.

"Three teams?" Markbreit asked, confused.

"Yeah," said Ryan. "We got the Arizona Cardinals, the New York Giants, and you seven assholes."

Chad thinks about Buddy Ryan now and, despite himself, smiles. Is it possible he's feeling nostalgia? Maybe. Maybe those were better days. This year, 1998, had been a brutal year for officials. Long ago, when he'd first started officiating, he'd been taught the definition of a good football game: a game in which nobody noticed you. This year the definition had changed. You had a good game if you weren't on the front page of the *New York Times*. Oh, well. A lot would be addressed during the off-season: instant replay, full-time officials, age limits. None of that matters now. Carolina is breaking from their huddle. He has to stuff his recollections into his memory bank and *focus*, focus on the game and on his goal: getting to the Super Bowl.

Chad blows on his hands. It is damp and chilly this

afternoon, and the field squishes beneath his cleats. Three Com Stadium doesn't absorb rain well, and it had poured all night and much of the morning. The grass smells sweet, but Chad, a big man, is concerned about his footing. On the field before the game, he should've paid more attention to wet spots instead of showing J. J. Stokes pictures of his kids.

Focus. The Niners seem loose. Bryant Young is kidding around with Chris Doleman. They don't seem overly concerned about Carolina, even though Steve Young isn't playing. The Panthers aren't going anywhere, but Wesley Walls, Eric Davis, Kevin Greene, and especially William Floyd told Chad before the game that they had something to prove. Floyd had it in for Ken Norton, Jr., his former teammate.

"We gonna beat 'em," Floyd told Chad. "No way they're stopping me. No way. Got nobody on that team can stop me. Not even Norton."

Chad laughed. "Whatever you say."

"I'm gonna go over there right now and tell him," Floyd said and jogged toward the Carolina side of the field.

Now, two hours later, Chad sticks his whistle into the corner of his mouth and leans in as Steve Beuerlein hands the ball to William Floyd.

It's the *sound* that you miss on TV, the sound that separates football from every other sport. The crack of plastic exploding into bone, hard rubber ramming into rock-hard muscle, the pounding, the crunching, men's grunts and breaths whooshing out. *"Ohhhmmmm,"* you hear, musical almost, religious nearly, and above it all the bruising roar of the crowd. The chill makes it all louder.

Floyd ducks his helmet and burrows into the line. He's met head-on by Norton and Young, who crash down on him.

Chad breaks for the play at the snap. The crowd noise hurtles down like thunder. Chad ends the play with his voice, darting into the pile of upended Panthers and twisted Franciscans: "Hey, hey, it's over! Play's over!" The ball squirts out of the pile, out of Floyd's fingers, and into Chad's awaiting palm. The players know Chad's style. He rarely blows his whistle. It's too impersonal. He wants the players to hear his voice, to know he's there. He believes that it makes the players feel that the game is under control.

"Second down!" Chad shouts.

Floyd, shaking his head, getting no more than two yards for his trouble, walks slowly back to his huddle.

"You take that shit out of *my* house!" Norton taunts.

Chad glares at him. Norton ignores him, races down the line, and looks over the offense as Carolina breaks out of their huddle.

"Pass!" Norton screams over Beuerlein's cadence. "It's a pass!" He turns all the way around, alerting Lee Woodall, the outside linebacker, and Darnell Walker, the left corner.

The Panthers' offensive line breaks backward, and sure enough, Raghib "Rocket" Ismail is slanting up the middle, right at Chad. Chad steps back, but Rocket keeps coming at full speed. He's using the umpire as a pick! The plan is to run the defender at Chad, then streak by and catch the quick pass up the middle.

The thing is, Chad *owns* the meat grinder and he doesn't want Rocket or anyone else in *his* house. As Rocket blows by, Chad lowers his shoulder and levels him. Rocket hurtles backward as if he's been shot. He flops into the soggy turf. Shaken, Rocket scrambles to locate who nailed him, expecting to see Norton. The only one around is the umpire. Chad turns casually away to watch the play unfold. Beuerlein, seeing Rocket on the ground, floats a pass toward Wesley Walls, the tight end. Walls, wearing a cast on his left wrist, snags the ball one-handed and tucks it in against his clump of plaster. He lowers his head as he's tackled upfield for a first down.

The Rocket lifts himself up and studies Chad Brown. The umpire is big, six-feet-five, 250 pounds, and even in stripes he looks formidable among these twenty-two behemoths in helmets and pads. Rocket opens his mouth, perhaps to complain, but complain to whom? The official? Shit. The official's the one who just clocked him.

"First down!" Chad bellows. Rocket jogs back to his huddle.

Chad is surprised at how aggressively Carolina has come out. They're attacking and pressing, knocking the Niners back on their heels. Beuerlein hands off again to Floyd. Norton leaps over the man trying to block him and hurls himself into Floyd. Floyd's head snaps back as Norton drives him into the ground.

"*Fuck!*" a voice shouts. Norton's? Floyd's? Impossible to tell.

Then Norton shouts, "Don't bring that shit to me!"

Floyd points a finger at Norton. "That the best you got? We be comin' at you all day long. Gonna drop you, baby, drop you!"

It's early, three downs into the game, but Chad's between them.

"Now, we're gonna *communicate*. None of that talk, hear? No trash. Just play the game." And like the referee he is, he pushes them apart. Floyd bounces into his huddle while Norton raises his arms to the crowd, trying to incite them into a first-quarter frenzy.

Chad digs in. Beuerlein takes the snap and drops back. He lofts a beautiful spiral down the left sideline. Mushid Muhammad glides under it, gathers it in, and is shoved out of bounds after a thirty-three-yard gain. Even though it's not his play and the wideout is not his man,

Chad turns and watches, for support. Last year in Arizona, against the Redskins, he made a call on a similar play. Jake "The Snake" Plummer scrambled out of the pocket and headed upfield. Plummer was hit but pulled away from the tackler and kept running. Chad thought he saw the Snake's knee touch the ground. He blew the play dead with his whistle. It was a questionable call, since he was out of position, and it cost Arizona a touchdown. Replays showed later that Plummer never went down. Arizona went on to lose the game and see their play-off hopes dashed. Chad hasn't blown his whistle since.

Carolina's now on the move. Another pass play to Muhammad. A slant to Rocket. Another first down. Then two stalled running plays to Fred Lane and an incomplete pass.

The field goal unit comes on. Chad, as umpire, stands between the two teams, waiting for Ed Hochuli, the referee, the man in charge, to give the word.

The teams in place, Hochuli says, "OK."

Chad backs toward his position behind the defense. The field goal's a chip shot, about a thirty-five-yarder. The snap is down, the kick is up, and . . . *blocked!*

Screaming. Panic. Confusion. It's like LA during a shaker. But here we have twenty-two football players running around looking for something to do. When in doubt, hit somebody. Or shout instructions: "Fall on it!" "Pick it up!" "Run with it!" "Lateral it!" "It's dead!" "It's alive!" But the most telling shout is a wail from John Kasay, the Carolina kicker, and someone screaming, "Goddam*sonofaBITCH*!" The ball skitters a few yards away, and a 300-pound 49er falls on it with the force of a side of a mountain collapsing on a shack. Hochuli whips out his arm, signaling a first down, and nearly takes out Kasay's eye as he passes by him, head down, mumbling rapidly and inaudibly like Dustin Hoffman in *Rain Man,* and behind him the cursing continues: "Motherfuckinggoddamn*shit*!" On the Carolina sideline, the special teams' coach, arms wide apart, howls, "What the hell was that? Who had that guy?"

TV time-out. The officials get to breathe. Chad takes off his hat, mops his head with his hand, and is face-to-face with Rocket Ismail.

"You gave me a *hit*, man."

"Little guy like you, it's best to stay out of the meat grinder," Chad suggests.

"Bad enough I gotta deal with the defense. Now I gotta deal with the umpire, too?"

Chad snickers.

Rocket doesn't crack a smile. He's got something on his mind: "I gotta ask you, man." Rocket clears his throat. He's nervous. "Did you play in this league?"

"Yeah, I did." Chad speaks slowly, gently, in a soft baritone. There remains a bit of southern lilt; he grew up in Dallas. The rhythm reminds you of Bill Cosby.

"Were you a linebacker?"

"No. Defensive end and offensive tackle."

Rocket nods, validated. He knew it. "Who'd you play for?"

"Pittsburgh Steelers, Houston Oilers, New Orleans Saints. It was a while ago. . . ." Chad's voice trails off.

"What do you like better, this or playing?"

"You kiddin'? This is way more fun. It's great having the whole world hate you. I love having everybody screaming at me every week on TV, in the papers, on the talk shows."

Rocket nods solemnly. "I hear you."

Chad regards Rocket. "Don't take me so seriously," he says. "I love officiating; I really do. I love being the man in the middle. Wish I got me some of that money they throw at you guys, though."

"It's different times, man," Rocket says.

"Yeah. A lot different."

"But you *made* it. You got to play in the National Football League, and that is really cool."

"It *is* cool. Course, I wasn't a superstar like you."

Now Rocket laughs. Chad takes a moment. He looks down at Rocket Ismail, so much younger, eagerly hanging on his every word, an impressionable kid soaking up the wisdom of the wise elder. If this were more than a television time-out, he'd tell the kid the story of his life. *Ah, what the hell,* thinks Chad. *I can at least start the story.*

"When I was a kid, all I thought about was football. I ate it, drank it, and went to sleep holding a football, under a picture of Sam Huff. Number 70. He was before your time."

"Heard of him, though," offers Rocket.

"He was my idol. And playing in the National Football League was my dream." Chad sighs. "It was the only thing I ever wanted to do. . . ."

His mind flashes back to a scene just a couple of months ago. It is a kids' birthday party at his house. His twin boys, Trent and Devin, are turning nine. They are standing over two burning forests of candles on two separate birthday cakes. Chad circles slowly behind them, squinting into the lens of a video camera. He's being artistic here, improvising a Scorsese-like tracking shot. Of course, no one will appreciate his artistry; he's sure it'll end up being his secret. His job is merely to record the precious moments of his sons' lives. By default, he's the family documentarian. These tapes, the constantly expanding film library, lie now in stacks on a shelf in his closet to be viewed at a later time in both amazement and embarrassment, depending on who's watching.

We never recorded our lives, thinks Chad. *We just lived them and relied on our memories. . . .*

2
KING OF THE STREET

The year is 1960. It's a hot Dallas day, a Tuesday, around noon, and a dozen schoolboys are playing tackle football in a vacant lot about a mile from Chad Brown, Sr.'s liquor store. It's a defiant gesture. The kids are supposed to be in school. Twelve-year-old Chad Brown doesn't care. He's doing what he does best and loves most: playing football. Besides, he's been challenged. His team, comprised exclusively of boys living on his home street, Macon Street, has been challenged by another team from nearby Harding Street. Harding claims they've got the best street team in South Dallas. Interesting. Macon claims the same thing.

It's early. There's no score. So far there's been a torrent of taunts and trash talk but not much football. Chad Brown, the Macon quarterback, gestures toward his team, waves them into a huddle around him. Towering above them, he studies the Harding Street defense. He senses something. A weakness. Their sudden fear. He keeps looking at them, his tongue clicking disapproval. The Harding Street boys shift positions, shout instructions to one another. They're suddenly uncomfortable, even intimidated. Their edge is certainly gone. Chad grins, a wide, confident grin that explodes into the neon smile that would get him out of so many scrapes in his life and into so many jams.

But that day his smile masked a mind whipping rapidly through the Macon Street playbook, a twelve-year-old's repertoire of fly patterns, bootlegs, and scrambles. He glanced at his brother, Ron, two years younger, his eyes large with expectation. Everyone knew that Chad would invent the proper play. He knelt down, dusted the ground with his palm, and smoothed out the dirt so he could draw. His thumb bumped a piece of broken glass. He tossed it away, out-of-bounds.

"Ronnie, go deep down the left sideline. Earl, cut over the middle. The rest of you, block somebody. If you're open, I'll hit you. Otherwise, I'll run."

They nodded. No questions asked. What Chad said made perfect sense. He spoke evenly, with assurance. No ego, just fact. The timbre of his voice, even more than his words, said clearly, *Follow me and we'll win.*

He drifted back about five yards away from center. In these games, every play came out of the shotgun. Chad took the snap and stepped up, then pumped twice toward the left sideline. Ronnie ran head-down, looking for an opening, but a tall, gangly kid had him covered, hell, had him *smothered.* Chad checked the middle. Earl was on his ass. A Harding kid powered through the line and wrapped his arms around Chad's waist. Chad tossed him off like a sweater. Then he tucked the ball into the crook of his arm and, with a move copied from Jim Brown in a game he had seen on TV, twisted away from two Harding kids and bolted up the right sideline. It was really no surprise. Everyone in that empty lot knew it was coming. To stop Macon, you had to stop Chad Brown, and that was pretty damn impossible.

Two kids to beat. A stocky kid who tried to hit him low. Chad ran right through him. No pads, no helmet. A *crunch*, a groan. That had to hurt. Now the other one, a solid kid, older, their best player. He had some form, some skills, and Chad actually thought he might have a shot at high school ball someday, if he had half a brain, a little luck, and didn't run with the wrong kids. The kid whacked Chad's legs with his shoulder and put all his weight into them. Chad teetered for a moment, then, using his free hand to balance himself, stiff-armed the kid hard, *wham,* and dashed away, toward the makeshift end zone, marked by a battered cardboard wine carton on one side and someone's torn shirt on the other. It was now a footrace. But no one could catch Chad. He streaked into the end zone and flipped the ball to his brother, Ron, who met him on the other side. There was no celebration in the end zone then. No victory dance. In 1960, Billy "White Shoes" Johnson was two years old and nobody had heard of the "Dirty Bird."

The game wasn't close. It never really was close when Chad played. He dominated. Today was especially rewarding. He and his boys had been put to the test. They took on Harding Street and didn't just beat them. They *scorched* them. After the losers walked off the vacant lot in defeat, their faces bloodied, bodies bruised, clothes ripped and muddied, Chad, feeling on top of the world, decided on this day of transgression to press his luck. What the hell. He was on a roll. And he was in the mood for plums.

The best plums around were in easy reach, right on Macon Street. They hung teasingly from a neighbor's plum tree. The only problem was the old lady who lived there. She didn't believe in sharing. It was her tree, her yard, her plums. Hers and hers alone. To Chad and the neighborhood kids, this made the fruit seem all the more juicy. It wasn't that difficult to walk away with a few of the forbidden fruit. All you had to do was climb the tree, fill your pockets with plums, and get the hell out of there. Chad and Ron had been caught a couple of times, but that was months ago. The memories of their punishments had faded into oblivion, becoming anecdotes, real or imagined, with which to regale their friends. Macon

Street rites of passage, evidence of manhood.

In the first story, the old lady awakened from her afternoon nap and found Chad dangling from the biggest tree limb, his pockets bulging with plums. She screamed, then arrived at the Browns' front door, threatening to call the police. The second story, the funny one, was the one Chad loved to tell, because it involved Ron. Chad's little brother, entwined in twigs ten feet up, stretched out toward an exquisitely plump plum at the end of a branch and fell out of the tree, nearly landing on the old lady's dozing mutt.

These incidents, fictional or forgotten, were not on Chad's mind as he approached the plum tree. The Macon Street boys hesitated as Chad directed them to start climbing. He was bigger, stronger, and, therefore, in charge. Besides, he promised, he'd already cased the old lady's house. She was downtown shopping. They were safe. As long as they made the heist quick and didn't alert the rest of the neighbors with their noise, they were golden. To prove his point, the boss struck first. Chad scrambled up the tree. He twisted a plum off a branch, held it up in his hand, and waved it triumphantly at his boys.

They were gone. In their place were two men Chad recognized as friends of his father's. A slow-motion instant replay of Chad Senior rolling up his sleeves and getting down to business on his son's ass began playing in his head. This good Tuesday was making an abrupt turn down a bad highway.

At home, an hour later, Chad Senior regarded his twelve-year-old son. As usual, the spanking hurt like hell. But this time Chad Senior's heart wasn't in it as much as his hand.

"Playing hooky, stealing," he said in a monotone. "Damn it, Chad, when are you gonna learn?"

Chad Brown, Sr., shook his head in frustration. He

was starting to wonder whether these whippings were working. He had no hard evidence that his message was piercing his son's thick, stubborn hide.

"I hate doing this, Chad. But it's for your own good."

Chad Senior sighed. He was hating the sound of his own clichés.

"I just want you take school seriously," he pleaded. He swallowed hard, then said softly, "Chad, listen to me. I want you to have it better than I did."

That night, Chad Senior dropped Chad off at his mother's house. Chad's parents were divorced when he was five. His mom, Everdee Battee, was thin and athletic, an outstanding runner in high school. She was past spanking Chad, which, she realized, never seemed to change his behavior anyway.

"We have to talk, Chad," she began as she dished out dinner.

This wasn't good. Clearly, the news of his latest crime spree had spread.

"You're *looking* for trouble, Chad. Why do you do these things?"

Chad scratched his head and looked down into his plate, to avoid his mother's eyes. She'd asked the wrong question. It wasn't *why* he did these things. It was why did he always get *caught*? He shifted his weight beneath the table and settled in. He knew that his mom was just getting warmed up.

"Chadwick, you might think life is all fun and games, but it isn't. It's hard work. You're gonna find that out someday and it's gonna come as a shock. Now," she said, shifting gears, "You are going to study hard and make something of yourself. Look what happens to the kids who don't take school seriously and who drop out. You're only twelve, but you have to think *ahead*, think about your future. I want you to have a dream, then work toward making that dream come true. Think big. Then we'll come up with a plan. Let's start with your goals. What are your goals, Chad?"

Chad silently poked his peas with his fork. He wasn't sure which was more painful, his father's spankings or his mother's preaching.

"I mean it, Chad," his mom insisted. "I want you to think of a goal for yourself."

Later, back at home, in the room he shared with his brother, Chad lay on his bed and stared at the ceiling. Dreams. Goals. A plan. He was *twelve*. His goal was to play as much street football as possible and keep his crown as King of the Neighborhood. *Not what my mom had in mind? OK, fine. How's this? Here's a good one for you. I'm going to become a superstar in the National Football League, like Sam Huff. That's my dream.*

Big enough for you?

3
BIGASS

Marvin Daniels, football coach of Lincoln High School, was built like a tank and was just as tough. A former college linebacker, Daniels knew football. He knew the game, and he knew how to compete. He also knew how to bust your ass in practice.

Which was what he was doing to Chad Brown right now.

Daniels was standing over him, screaming, his face contorted into one frightening frown, as Chad, in full uniform, helmet, and pads, his brow furrowed in pain, crawled on his forearms down the middle of the football field. This drill was called the crab walk, an innocent name for fifty yards of sheer torture.

"Come on, All-City!" Daniels screamed at Chad. "Let's go! Faster! Come onnn! You All-City or All-*Shitty?*"

Chad reached the fifty and the coach blew his whistle. Chad collapsed. He glanced up at Marvin Daniels and detected a glimmer of a grin.

"You tough, Chad. That's good. You need to be tough. Now take a break, you earned it."

Chad sucked in waves of air and looked at the kid next to him, who was also lying in a heap, gasping for air. He was a sophomore, a running back named Duane Thomas. The same Duane Thomas who would later star for the Dallas Cowboys and eventually take on Tom

Landry and the Cowboys' front office in a legendary contract dispute. Thomas, crunched into a crab on his hands and knees, was then and would be in the future quiet, confident, talented, and aware that everyone around him in a suit wanted a piece of that talent for himself.

"OK, babies, break's over! Crab walk into the end zone, girls!"

Daniels blew his whistle inches away from Chad's ear. Chad lifted himself up into a proper crab walk position and, with Daniels shadowing him like a detective, crawled another agonizing fifty yards into the end zone. The coach was making a statement. If he treated his star player like shit, he could treat everybody else worse.

After the crab walk, Daniels allowed his players to collect themselves for at least twenty seconds. Then he blew his whistle again.

"OK! Touches! Start at the fifty! Show 'em, Chad! Go!"

In sheer pain and utter disbelief, Chad lifted himself up and hustled back to the fifty-yard line. He touched the hash mark, ran back into the end zone, turned back, and sprinted all the way to the twenty-five-yard line on the far side of the field. Daniels blew the whistle and the rest of the team sprinted after Chad. He was gasping, sweating, swearing, and wondering whether or not the abuse his body was enduring was really worth it.

That afternoon, Chad walked home with a group of his friends. They walked quietly for a block; then Chad, shaking his head, blurted, "Sometimes I just feel like quitting."

"He's just messin' with you, Chad," one of his friends said. "Using you as an example. I think you're one of his favorites."

"Oh, yeah. He's crazy about me. That's why he kicks my butt every afternoon from three to five. Good thing

I'm one of his favorites, otherwise he might treat me *bad*."

"I'm serious, Chad."

Chad considered this. "Well, maybe. I'll tell you what though, putting my body through all this, I wonder if it's worth it."

Tony, one of his closest friends, nodded as he pulled a cigarette out of a pack. He lit it and inhaled deeply. "I know what you mean, brother. You gotta take care of your body."

Chad stared at Tony as he blew smoke rings.

"What? It's my afternoon smoke. I have a lot of stress in my life. This relaxes me. You know that. You smoke, right, Chad?"

Chad looked off. "Sure."

The others all laughed.

"What's so funny? I *smoke*. All the time. You've just never *seen* me smoke. I smoke in secret 'cause it's against team rules."

Tony nodded. "Uh-huh."

"Give me one of those." Chad pointed at Tony's cigarettes.

Tony shrugged and held the pack out to him. Chad reached in and, with a flourish, yanked out a Camel. All eyes were on him.

"What are you-all staring at?"

"Nothin.' " Tony shrugged again and handed him a book of matches.

Chad fumbled with it, pulled out a match, and tried to light it. He tried three times. The match tip broke off. "Damn matchbook's wet," he said.

Tony offered Chad the lit end of his butt. Chad dragged on it, sucked in the smoke. He blew it out instantly. He felt as if a car's exhaust pipe had been shoved down his throat. A moment later, he was on a boat in the middle of a storm. He was green, puke green, and dizzy as hell. He started to cough. Not just a quiet, semi-annoying cough, but a phlegm-filled bronchial hack that exploded through his chest with the force of someone dying.

"Not my brand," he wheezed. He was as green as a golf course.

The others turned away to avoid bursting into group hysterics. "I'm under a lot of stress, too," Chad said and sucked down another nauseating drag. The back of his throat felt as if it were packed with soot. But he was not about to show his friends anything but cool. He kept the cigarette dangling from his lip the same way the older guys did when they came out of his father's liquor store.

Without a doubt, thought Chad, *this has to be the dumbest habit in the world.* He made himself a promise: *This is my first and last cigarette. I'll turn the corner, stamp it out. Maybe I'll even confess. Tell them I don't smoke. Never have in my life, never will again.*

He turned the corner. Walking toward him was another group of kids from Lincoln. Tony waved. They stopped and stared at Chad Brown, football player and role model. They pointed at him and laughed.

"Damn." Chad opened his mouth. The cigarette parachuted to the pavement.

"You're awright, Chad," Tony said. "I don't think they saw you."

The next afternoon at football practice, the thirty members of the Lincoln High School football team stood in two lines, about four feet apart, facing each other. The first player, standing sheepishly with a large wooden paddle in his hand, was Duane Thomas.

Coach Daniels walked through the line silently, his hands linked behind his back. Then he addressed his players like Patton addressing his troops.

"Discipline. You cannot play football without it. Now. What exactly is discipline?"

He waited. The team knew he wasn't expecting an answer. He was just pausing for effect. He wanted his words to be momentous.

"Rules. That's what discipline is. Very simple. Rules. But not just any rules. *My* rules. You have to follow my rules, or you can't play on my team. You wanna break my rules, you have two choices. One, go home. Or two, pay the price."

Daniels stopped at the very end of the line and stuck his nose an inch away from Chad's face. "This man broke one of my rules. So. What's it going to be, Chad Brown? Number one or number two? You going home? Or you gonna pay?"

What surprised Daniels and the rest of the team was that Chad didn't answer right away; he hesitated. It frankly surprised Chad, too. He stood on the grassy field behind his high school and thought through both choices, weighing them carefully. In his mind, at that moment, he was deciding between football and freedom. There was no knee-jerk response, no automatic answer. A part of him knew instinctively that he was making a life decision, a choice that would not be without its share of pain.

Finally, Chad swallowed and said, almost inaudibly, "I'll pay the price."

"*WHAT?*" shouted Daniels.

"I said I'll pay the price."

"Damn right you will."

Daniels looked pleased. He spun away from Chad and walked briskly toward Duane Thomas. The coach flicked his forefinger against the hard wood of the paddle.

"Rule number one!" he shouted. "No smoking. Ever. Now go through the line, Chad. And the rest of you, don't hold back. I catch you holding back it'll be *your* ass. Got that? Oh and, Chad, see me after practice."

Chad wanted to protest, "One time! That's all it was. One *time*! Why do I always get caught?"

Whack! Duane Thomas took a full swing at Chad's butt. Stinging pain shot through Chad's rump and legs. Thomas passed the paddle to the next player. He whaled at Chad. *Wham!* The next player took the paddle. *Swack!* One by one, the thirty of them, his teammates, wound up and swung away and pounded on his ass as if it were a piñata. Tears welled up, but he fought them back.

About an hour after practice, Chad, in his school clothes, knocked politely at Marvin Daniels's door. "Come on in, Chad." Daniels was calmer, more personable, now. "Sit down," he offered.

"I can't."

"Oh, yeah."

"I don't smoke, Coach. It was a onetime thing. I was just trying to be cool."

Daniels waved him away. "I figured it was something dumb like that. I had no choice, Chad. I had to make an example of you."

This time Chad nodded. He understood.

The coach shrugged and settled into his chair. "I'm getting calls about you."

"Calls?"

"Yeah. From most of the small colleges in the area. And all the black schools. Got three today. Howard, Grambling, Texas Southern. They all want you."

"They do? I didn't know—"

"You do now. So, Chad, what about your future?"

"Well, Coach, to tell you the truth, I haven't given it much thought."

"You better start. You're going to have some choices to make. That's something a lot of kids don't have. So, what do you think? Any idea where you want to go?"

"I don't know. I wasn't counting on a lot of choices. What do you think?"

"Well, it depends. You have to decide if you want to go to a big pond and be a little fish or go to a little pond and be a bigass fish."

He stood up, draped his coach's whistle around his neck.

"Myself, I like being the bigass."

4
JUMPING OVER THE MOON

Chad wavered between two little ponds: Arizona State College in Flagstaff and Corpus Christi University. Ultimately, he decided on Corpus Christi because of an irresistible presentation in his father's living room by the Corpus Christi football coach. The coach reminded Chad of a used car salesman. Chad decided not to be too judgmental and to look past the man, at the product he was selling—the exciting new football program, the campus, and the opportunity for him to excel.

Corpus Christi University was a tiny college with a big-time dream. The coach explained that this was going to be the first year of its football program and Chad Brown was going to be the cornerstone of the team. With Chad as the foundation of their entire program, they would recruit players who would complement Chad. He was the glue, the anchor, the Man.

The coach, whose name is long forgotten, clicked through dozens of seductive slides projected in living color on Chad Senior's living room wall. *Click.* Here is a cluster of ivy-covered buildings, giving the campus an East Coast charm. *Click.* Check out the library, student union, fraternity row, and dining commons with not one, but *two* gourmet chefs. *Click.* That's Corpus Christi Pond, right in the center of campus. The football team will spend the bulk of their study time here, when they're not in the library, because this is where the coeds like to sunbathe. *Click.* An artist's rendering of the new fifty-thousand-seat football stadium. Everything state-of-the-art. And wait just two years, Chad, when Corpus Christi will take on Division I state rivals like Texas and Texas A & M. *Click.* Rolling hills, just off campus. Hiking trails, picnic areas, breathtaking views of the valley. Take a break from your studies and bask in nature's glory. *Click.* A view of the Gulf of Mexico, five minutes away. Fishing, boating, water-skiing, or just an ideal spot to watch the sunset. *Click.* Is that . . . ? Yes! That's Roger Staubach! Grinning. With his arm around *me!* If Corpus Christi were around when he went to college, he would have enrolled here instead of the Naval Academy. But he's a huge supporter of the football program, and you know what that means? *Click.* You guessed it. The Cotton Bowl! By your senior year, Chad.

Click, click, click.

Of course, it was all bullshit. There was no pond. No ivy. No rolling hills. No library, for that matter. The Gulf was two hours away. The football team practiced in a parched field. And there was no evidence anywhere that Roger Staubauch had ever even *heard* of Corpus Christi.

The first day, Chad sat alone in the dining commons and regarded his lunch, a brown stringy blob floating in an unidentified murky liquid that might very well have been plucked from an oil slick. "I guess the two gourmet chefs are off today," Chad muttered.

A young man his age sat down next to him. He smiled. "Hey."

"Hey," answered Chad.

The young man extended his hand. "I'm Jim Bob Rutledge."

"Chad Brown."

"I'm pretty excited about going to school here. How about you?" Jim Bob asked, digging into his mystery lunch.

"Oh, yeah. Very excited."

"Umm. This is good. They got two gourmet chefs here."

"I heard."

"Yep. They recruited me to play football. I was second-team All-City linebacker, Jefferson High in Houston."

"Great."

"Yep. They got a new football program here, they're starting it up."

"I heard that, too."

"Yep. They're building the whole deal around me. Ain't that something? I coulda gone other places, but when the coach decided to make me the cornerstone of the whole program, I couldn't turn him down. I mean, could you?"

"No," said Chad, his stomach sinking. "I couldn't turn him down either. Nobody could."

"Exactly. What do you call a guy like that? There's a name for him . . ."

A slick piece of shit? Chad thought to himself.

"A visionarian. Yep, that's it," said Jim Bob. "So, they recruit you for basketball?"

"Hockey," Chad said as he got up.

I'm going to give it a chance, thought Chad later in his dorm room. *I'm no quitter.*

He gave it three days. In that time, the used car salesman/football coach dropped his slick veneer and became a screaming, saliva-spitting, jersey-grabbing tyrant. Instead of the typical two-a-day workouts, he forced the fledgling football team into three-a-days, unheard of for freshmen. "It's an attempt to jump-start the football program," he explained.

When Chad wasn't at practice, he walked to classes, shielding his eyes with his books from the swirling, biting dust that covered the campus. *Cotton Bowl, my ass.*

The only bowl they're ever going to is the Dust Bowl.
When he did manage to squint through the brown haze
that hung over the college, he encountered a sea of snarl-
ing faces. Unlike the *Cheers* bar, this was the place
where *nobody* knew your name. They didn't seem too
happy about your looks, either.

Lonely, depressed, and desperate, Chad remembered
there was another choice: Arizona State College. It had
been a close second, rejected primarily because Chad, a
homebody, then and now, didn't want to be so far away
from his family and friends. Three of his high school
teammates had enrolled there, and Coach Daniels had
thought, all things considered, it actually was a better fit
for Chad than Corpus Christi. At the end of the third
day and ninth football practice, and after he'd met thirty
other football players around whom the new program
was going to be built, Chad decided that he could be
called a quitter all day long; he didn't care—he just
wanted to get the hell out of there. He phoned Leo Haberlack, the head football coach at Arizona State College, and genuinely and honestly admitted that he'd
made a mistake.

He dreaded dialing the phone, but it turned out to be
the easiest phone call he'd ever made. In retrospect, it
was probably too easy. Haberlack offered him an immediate spot on the Arizona State College football team,
accompanied by a full scholarship.

Chad shoved all of his earthly belongings into his two
suitcases, and within an hour he was gone, escaping
from the Corpus Christi campus as fast as his legs would
carry him. Suddenly he heard a car pull up behind him
on the red dirt road leading to the main highway. It
thudded to a stop. The door opened and a man came
running up behind him. The coach/used car salesman.

"You can't leave!" he screamed.

Chad just kept walking.

"You come back here!"

Chad ignored him.

"I'm telling you, you better not walk off this campus! I know a lawyer!"

Chad picked up the pace, leaving the man standing in a cloud of red clay dust. His face red as the Red River, blue veins popping out of his neck like a relief map, the coach screamed, "Chad Brown, I promise you this! As long as I'm alive, you will never play a down of college football!"

Chad broke into a run. The guy was scaring him. What if he was right? After all, Chad's entire college football career so far consisted of a grand total of three terrible days, nine brutal practices, and a pack of lies.

It would get worse.

Arizona State College, in 1966, was more than a different world to Chad Brown. It was a different planet.

It wasn't that way immediately. At first, it seemed like old home week. Chad was met on campus by three of his high school teammates. They escorted him onto the practice field, where he arrived with a résumé popping with impressive credentials: first-team All-City defensive lineman and third-team All-State defensive lineman. But things soured fast.

Arizona State College was a small college with a big-time football program. The two-a-day practices were brutal and intense, the coaches unrelenting, the competition fierce.

And, for the first time in his life, he was aware of something else. A noxious, oozing fume that dogged him at every turn.

Racism.

It was pervasive and constant. Chad could feel its presence always, like a low-level hum off an electrical current. He encountered it everywhere: the library, the student store, restaurants in town, local movie theaters. He felt it on campus as he walked with his black teammates among the student population, a diverse mixture of hippies, conservatives, and cowboys.

Playing football became his salvation. It was an outlet, an avenue in which he could express his anger, fear, frustration, and, increasingly, his unhappiness.

He never would have dreamed that Flagstaff, Arizona, would turn out to be the end of the earth, the ultimate shock to his system. It was amazing. Living his entire life in South Dallas, made up of almost all black faces, had lulled him into a false sense of security. Hell, a false sense of the *world*. He spent his days in South Dallas, on his street, in his neighborhood, feeling comfortable, safe, happy. The world out here in Flagstaff was, simply, white, and he was a visitor. An unwelcome visitor. A brother from another planet who'd crash-landed in the cold heart of the desert.

In mid-November, going to college and playing football began to become a burden. It was as if Chad had taken on two full-time jobs and neither was going particularly well. The fact that he was a highly recruited football player made no difference. In an effort to assimilate all student athletes, the school mandated that the football team would receive no special privileges or preferential treatment. A noble idea, perhaps, but unrealistic given both the everyday demands put on the football team and the racial climate. It was hard enough to blend in as a football player; it was impossible if you were a black football player.

To get through even the most ordinary day, a day that included surviving two football practices, suffering through classes, and squeezing in time for studying, the football team had to be creative. Meals were a special challenge. The problem was the team shared the cafeteria with the rest of the student population but didn't share the same dining hours. Lunch, for example, was served from 12 until 1:30, a direct conflict with football practice, which finished at 1:00. By the time the team showered, changed, and raced across campus to the cafeteria, lunch would be over. Assimilation or not, if the players didn't devise some sort of system for meals, they simply would never eat.

Thus the idea of a meal leader was born. Each day a different football player, the meal leader, was given the assignment to assure that the team got their turn in the cafeteria. The meal leader would leave practice early, shower before the other players, sprint to the cafeteria, cut into the line, and reserve spots for the rest of the team. If lunch service looked like it was about to shut down, the meal leader would begin loading food onto trays. It wasn't a perfect system, but the other students went along with the program, willingly allowing the football players to cut in.

Chad's turn as meal leader occurred the week before Thanksgiving. The season was winding down. He dashed off the practice field, showered in a second, threw on his clothes, rushed into the cafeteria, and found a place in line. He stretched his head toward the cafeteria workers, women in hair nets shoveling muck behind metal serving stations, and saw that, timewise, he was OK. As he caught his breath, he began to reflect on what had been a tremendously difficult transition. He vowed to get himself more together next semester, take better care of his time. Organize. He would attack his work, put in extra hours in the library. He sighed. Looked around. He really didn't want to face his true feelings. Yes, he could do all these things, start from scratch with a new attitude, renewed determination, all that. But he was homesick and out of place. He missed his friends and family. The truth, the deep truth, was that he hated it here.

Then he heard that hum.

He wasn't sure how long it had been going on, but he became aware now that someone behind him was staring at him. Chad bolted out of his reverie and saw a tall, wiry cowboy with, he swore, a red neck, staring into his eyes. The cowboy was as tall as he was.

"What the hell do you think you're doin'?" the cowboy asked evenly.

Chad took a breath. He didn't know whether he should answer. The football players' meal system was well-known on campus. No one had ever questioned it before. The line moved forward. Chad moved with it.

"You just come in here and cut in line? Is that what you do?"

The cowboy didn't really want an explanation. Chad knew that. He had seen him before. Or his type. They'd move through the campus in clusters, bobbing like whitecapped waves, on Chad's periphery. He would avoid making eye contact with them. And they with him. In fact, they would avoid him altogether. If Chad and his friends sat at their table, they would move away.

The cowboy pushed into Chad with his shoulder.

Hummmm.

"The thing is, I'm on the football team." Chad decided to explain softly.

"I know. Nigger."

The word, simply, burned.

He wanted to run. He wanted to scream. And, for a moment, he wanted to cry. Yet the strongest, clearest emotion he felt, to his surprise, was failure. He knew, now, that he'd reached an end. At that moment, in this cafeteria, in this hated place, Chad saw the closing of a book, felt the slamming of a door.

He said nothing. He curled his lip and pressed it against his teeth.

After the meal, Chad waited outside the cafeteria.

The cowboy came out of the building. No words were said. Chad went for him, fists flailing in fury, and the cowboy went down. Blood spurting. Dust rising. Shooting pain up the side of his hand. All a blur. It was too much. All of it. Too much. Too damn much. And, as Chad walked away from the figure on the ground, it was also not enough.

Not nearly enough.

Chad returned home to South Dallas. The incident appeared in the newspaper. The story avoided any mention of race. Instead, the article focused on the fact that Chad Brown, local high school football hero, was dismissed from Arizona State College for fighting. The three weeks from Thanksgiving until Christmas, 1966, were a mixture of raw emotion and reunion. Chad spent almost every night with his friends and almost every day trying to placate his parents.

"What now, Chad?" was the question seared into his head by everyone from Everdee, to Chad Senior, to Coach Daniels. Chad's promise to his parents that he would get a college education and his dream of becoming a professional football player had become a blinking red hold button. He relived the incident in Flagstaff, tried to replay the moment. One word had changed his life.

"You shouldn't have done it," a friend said to him one night. "It wasn't worth it."

Chad had no argument. But, silently, he also had no regret.

"But I did it. Now what am I going to do?" he wondered aloud.

The answer came in a phone call from Ernest Hawkins, head football coach at East Texas State University in Commerce. Hawkins had seen the story about Chad in a local newspaper. The article described Chad as talented and available. Hawkins wanted him.

At the beginning of January 1967, after his third college send-off in five months, Chad climbed aboard a bus to Commerce. A full scholarship awaited him the following September if everything worked out.

A young man, an assistant football coach, arrived at the bus station to meet Chad and drive him to campus. The man was an oddity among football coaches. He was rumpled, nervous, studious, working on his Ph.D. He was also white. Color, rarely a concern growing up, was now, Chad realized, an issue. As the car drove off toward a new chapter in his life, Chad thought about how drastically he had changed in sixteen weeks. He had been a quiet leader, yet accommodating to everyone, especially those in authority. He was not going to let this opportunity at East Texas State slip away, no matter what. But he wasn't going to sacrifice his self-respect, either.

"Heard good things about you, Chad. Looking forward to having you play football for us." The coach spoke in a nasal drone.

"I appreciate the call," Chad said sincerely. He studied the man. The inside of the car smelled as if it had just gone through a car wash. A tiny cardboard tree hung from the visor. Chad couldn't tell if the scent was antiseptic peppermint or emergency room evergreen.

"Let me ask you something," Chad said.

"Shoot."

"How many black athletes do you have on the football team?"

"*Black* athletes. Well, let's see." The coach shifted in his seat to get a better feel for the road and the question. "I'm going to say five. No. Six. Five or six."

"They all start?"

"Oh, yeah. They're all *good*. Real good."

Chad kept his eyes facing the blacktop in front of him. The coach cleared his throat. What a question. The freshman had knocked him back on his heels. The Ph.D. student was the one off-balance. He felt the need to right himself.

"See, Chad, here's the thing." The coach lowered his voice as if the two of them, alone in the scented car, could be overheard. "All the white athletes have to be able to jump up and touch the moon."

Chad took this in, then asked, "What about the black athletes?"

"They have to be able to jump *over* the moon."

There it was again. Rising in volume. Crackling louder. Unapologetic. Appearing in his own backyard, deep in the heart of Texas.

Hummmmm.

SECOND QUARTER
III

5
YOU SAY THERE'LL BE AN EVOLUTION. . . .

You've seen the photograph.

Three muscular men, two black, one white, all wearing nylon warm-ups, standing side by side in living black and white. All are Olympic champions, sprinters, representatives of their countries, yet the two black men are, in their own hearts and minds, outcasts.

The scene is the Awards Ceremony for the 200-meter dash at the 1968 Summer Olympics in Mexico City. The white man, Peter Norman from Australia, the silver medal winner, is on the left. "The Star-Spangled Banner" is playing, and Norman stands, respectfully, at attention. The two black men, Tommy Smith, center, winner of the gold, and John Carlos, right, the bronze medal winner, stand in utter defiance. Carlos is the bigger man, the one with the broader shoulders and the troubled eyes. In the photograph, he stands with his bronze medal draped around his neck, his head bowed, his right fist thrust straight into the sky.

The photograph today still moves you, angers you, threatens you, politicizes you, stirs you up. It expresses, remarkably, both a candid portrait of contempt and a celebration of black power. John Carlos could not, in good conscience, represent his country, a country that so many times, in so many ways, had turned its back on him.

John Carlos was twenty years old and married when

he arrived at East Texas State University by way of New York City. Smooth and strong, graceful and swift, he was the most gifted athlete Chad had ever seen.

"He could flat out *fly*," Chad remembers thirty-two years later with a smile.

At East Texas State, John Carlos was more than a runner; he was a mythic figure. One time, or so the story goes, competing in the 100-yard dash against the best sprinters in the world, Carlos tripped coming out of the starting blocks. He picked himself up, turned on his afterburner, and smoked the field, finishing the race in 9.3 seconds.

Carlos, the man, had a profound effect on Chad. Chad had never met anyone like him. John was a gifted athlete, but that was secondary. He was, first and foremost, a man. A black man. He was outspoken, brash, and completely intolerant of intolerance. He answered to no one, refused to be manipulated by a system designed to exploit him, and was nobody's fool. As a friend, he was as solid as his body. Chad spent hours listening to John's political views and observations of racism. Carlos opened Chad's eyes. He began to see his own life and the world around him from a different perspective.

The evolution of Chad Brown unleashed emotions in him that were complicated and conflicting. On the one hand, when it came to football, he had nothing but respect for Coach Ernest Hawkins. The more Chad practiced and played for Hawkins, the more he saw that he was developing into a top-notch lineman and a crucial piece of the East Texas State football program. Chad also knew that East Texas State enjoyed a national reputation, extraordinary for a small college. The word in the program was do what Hawkins says and good things will happen. The team *wins* and the best players, generally the ones who most embrace the system, get drafted into the National Football League. Chad counted at least four members of his graduating class, including himself, who were potential NFL draft picks.

On the other hand, Chad was slowly discovering that not all players under the system were created equal. Chad saw that passive-aggressive racism ran rampant on the football team. To begin with, racism dripped down the white sheet that announced the starting lineups. Mediocre white players were given the nod over superior black players. During the games, praise was heaped on white players when they made routine plays; black players were ignored when they made outstanding plays. If a white player made a mistake, he heard encouragement: "That's OK! You'll get 'em next time!" If a black player made a mistake, he was greeted with icy stares. When the team lost, all the black players were blamed. When the team won, usually because of the black players, it was called a team effort.

The football team had an insidious policy in place that kept the number of black players on the team to a minimum. This policy was called "stacking." When a black player arrived at East Texas, he would automatically be "stacked" behind another black player in the depth chart. A black player was never placed next to another black player, especially in the offensive or defensive line, regardless of his ability. If you were a black lineman, the only way you could replace the guy ahead of you in your stack was if he graduated, left school, or died.

"You've got to do something about this stacking shit," John Carlos said.

"Yeah? Like what?"

"I don't know. Challenge the system."

That was fine for John Carlos, but it wasn't Chad Brown's style. Chad was not prepared to do anything that would risk throwing away his football career. *Been there, done that,* thought Chad. He had to bide his time, use the ugliness that surrounded him on the football field to toughen him up, make him stronger. At least on campus, in the comfort of his black teammates and roommates, Chad felt physically safe.

Which was not the case off campus. Virulent racism was visible just a few miles away. When Chad and his roommates roamed off campus for a pizza or a movie, they would commonly drive by Ku Klux Klan cross burnings. To Chad, the sight was satanic, beyond frightening, beyond reason. It was a ritual of the insane, fiery evidence of a blind hatred so foreign to him that the first time he saw the night sky ablaze with the outline of a cross he could only stare openmouthed.

He threw himself into football. He had formulated a new goal, and he vowed to achieve it: he was determined to play in the National Football League. He hit the weight room hard. He pushed himself to the max; he *punished* himself. No pain, no gain. Chad gained. From a freshman weight of 210 pounds he bulked up to a senior size of 243 pounds.

Coach Hawkins embraced the *image* of Chad Brown to the outside world, especially to the press. The coach was a quote machine. Reporters buzzed around him like hungry hornets. When Chad was named the Lone Star Conference's Lineman of the Week, Hawkins said admiringly, "The offense couldn't block Brown and they couldn't run around him." The next season began with preseason predictions. Hawkins and Boley Crawford, the line coach, said, "Brown swallows up everything that comes his way. We just can't find a way to block him." Chad read the articles and laughed. Hawkins spoke of him with such high regard publicly when on the football field he rarely spoke to him at all.

From the very first whistle of his very first practice, Chad performed like a man possessed. He found a hidden accelerator somewhere deep inside himself and kept it pressed to the floor. Offense, defense, it didn't matter.

There was no slack time, no rest, and no letup. His work-out sessions served him well. Chad became a force. He was equally adept at leveling charging linemen and sacking the quarterback. When the season started, Hawkins and Crawford couldn't decide where Chad should play, offense or defense. The coaches finally realized they wanted all of him, all of the time, so they went for broke and started him on both sides of the ball. By his senior season, Chad had accumulated a stack of honors: East-man Kodak All-America team, NAIA All-American, UPI All-Texas, second-team All-Conference. Blocker or pass rusher, he was both feared and respected.

Being named a preseason Kodak All-American made Chad more visible on campus and put pressure on him to live up to his hype. Boley Crawford told Chad that pro scouts would start coming to East Texas State games, looking at him seriously for the upcoming NFL draft. Being an All-American, he would now be in the spotlight. He should work harder.

"This could be your only chance to get drafted. Make the most of it," Crawford said.

Chad took his advice. After practice, Chad would spend another hour on mechanics, especially working on his pass-blocking techniques. Then he'd run. He was setting an example. Other players joined the additional workouts. Chad was the Man.

As a reward for being named to the All-America team, Chad received a gift from his father—a brand-new 1967 ChevMrolet Malibu with a monster 396 cubic engine. Because he had the hottest wheels in his group, Chad was named designated driver. He didn't mind. He liked to drive and this machine could *kick.* Chad cruised through campus, radio blasting, his guys hanging out the windows. He didn't even mind getting stuck with nine o'clock classes. He could get up late. He had the 396 and he could *drive.* He'd pull into a faculty parking space, which required a permit that he didn't have, leave the car, go to class, come out fifty minutes later, pull the parking ticket off his windshield, and stuff it into the glove compartment with all the rest of his unpaid parking tickets. By the end of the year, Chad would accumulate close to twelve hundred dollars in parking tickets, which the university magically paid. Or ignored. Or fixed. He never knew. The advantage of being an All-American.

As Chad prepared for the football season, John Carlos prepared for the biggest track meet in the state, the famed Texas Relays, held in Austin. The East Texas State track team would leave for Austin the Friday before the relays. Friday morning, John Carlos's wife woke up ill. She was so sick that John insisted she check into the infirmary. As they sat in the waiting room, Chad and Carlos watched the track team pile into the team station wagon and take off.

"Don't you want to run in the relays?" asked Chad.

"More than anything," said Carlos. "But my wife, my family, come first. That's the way it is. That's the way it always should be."

"I'm sure she'll be fine, 'Los," said Chad.

"If she is, I'll go later."

"How? There goes your team in that station wagon."

"I see that."

"So how you gonna get to Austin?"

"I haven't figured that out yet."

John's wife was diagnosed with a slight case of food poisoning. She would have to spend the night in the infirmary. She gave John her blessing to run in the Texas Relays.

Six o'clock the next morning Chad burst into John's bedroom while John was still asleep.

"Come on, let's go," Chad said, "I gotta get back. I got a game today."

"What? Where we going?" John peered at him grog-gily.

"Where do you think? Austin."

"Austin? It's two hundred miles away. Take you three hours to get there, three to get back. You'll never make it."

"Have you been in my 396?"

"Of course I've been in your car."

"I don't have a car," Chad scoffed. "I have a rocket ship. Now let's go. Pack your bag."

John Carlos grinned. "It's already packed."

It wasn't close. Chad drove the way Carlos ran. Fast. Way over the speed limit. He deposited John Carlos in Austin, wished him luck, spun out, and sped back to Commerce, pulling into his parking space as casually as if he'd just come from the store.

Thirty-two years later, a point of contention remains. On the way to Austin, Chad was busted for speeding. A large white state trooper slapped Chad with his first moving violation. The difference was that the university wouldn't take care of a speeding ticket. That was between Chad and his father, who would not be pleased.

There is no arguing that Chad got the speeding ticket. The argument is *why?*

"Why?" asks Chad. "Why did I get the speeding ticket? I got it because I was *speeding*. The speed limit was maybe sixty-five, seventy, and I didn't get below eighty-five the whole way."

"That is not why he got the speeding ticket," insists John Carlos. "He drives like an old lady, then and now. The only reason he got the ticket was because a white state trooper saw two black dudes in a nice car on a Texas highway. Period. That's why he got the ticket."

John Carlos. Runner. Radical. Myth.

*   *   *

The annual NFL draft, televised live from Madison Square Garden on ESPN, has become, without a doubt, our nation's most bizarre television event. Every April, millions of die-hard football fans plunk themselves in front of their television sets for nine hours to watch Paul Tagliabue and Gene Washington stand at a podium and read names off index cards. These men are not exactly Billy Crystal and Robin Williams, but we don't care. We're watching the *draft*.

We've been waiting for this for weeks. In the interim, we've been glued to sports talk radio, listening to football experts gushing over prospects from the combines and the Senior Bowl. We've pored over dozens of mock drafts in newspapers and magazines. We are now desperate to know which players will be drafted when, how each team's needs will be filled, and we pray, after all this anticipation, when our favorite team makes its first-round pick, we don't find ourselves staring at our sets in horror, gasping, "*Who?*"

In 1969, the year Chad Brown became eligible for the NFL draft, it was a different story. The draft then was made up of eighteen rounds over two days. The entire draft-day hoopla consisted of college football players who had a notion they would be drafted sitting by the phone in their dorm rooms, waiting for the National Football League to call. There was no national ruckus, no mock drafts, no sports talk on the radio, no ESPN. If you were lucky enough to live in a big city or had access to a major newspaper, you might find the draft summarized the next day in the sports section. If not, around July 4 you could find your favorite team's draft picks listed in a football magazine.

Buoyed by a case of beer, East Texas State stars Chad Brown, Richard Houston, and Tom Black settled into Chad's dorm room. Chad placed the phone strategically in the center of the room, within easy reach of all of them. He turned on the radio to an all-news station that gave draft updates every half hour. They began the proceedings with a promise: for every round that passed without all of them being drafted, they each had to drink at least one beer. They popped open their first beer and toasted. Welcome to the 1969 NFL draft!

Houston, a wide receiver and Vietnam vet, figured to go first, perhaps as high as the third round. Black, another wide-out who "ran good routes," which meant he was slow and white, held a bunch of East Texas State receiving records but was hoping just to get drafted, period. Chad, who'd had a solid senior season, thought he could be picked by the sixth or seventh round. As his dream of playing in the National Football League was on the verge of becoming a reality, he began to feel nothing but sheer, unadulterated panic. You wouldn't know it. He lay coolly on his bed, made small talk, played an occasional hand of cards. The waiting was killing him. The phone stared haughtily back at him, solid, alone, silent. *If you watch it, it won't ring*, Chad reminded himself. He turned his back to it, a sign of defiance, nonchalance. But couldn't everyone hear the pounding of his heart?

Chad had every reason to believe the phone would ring, and ring by the seventh round at the latest. The Philadelphia Eagles, among other teams, had taken a good, hard look at him. They'd sent a scout to watch him work out at his old high school, Lincoln, as members of the high school team watched in awe. Chad did side-to-sides, backpedals, and rollovers and ran a forty. The Eagles seemed impressed, as did the Chargers and several other teams who would later put him through the same drill. It was all now a blur, as he looked at the phone out of the corner of his eye. *Nope. That wasn't the phone and there goes another round.* He popped open another beer.

Finally, the phone rang. Chad jumped. It was for Richard. The New York Giants were calling. They'd drafted him in the fourth round, a sincere show of confidence. Richard hung up the phone and screamed. Chad hugged him, then flopped back down on the bed. The phone. The damn phone. *Ring, damn you. Ring.*

It rang. It was for Chad. He had been drafted in the *third* round—by the Saskatchewan Wildcats of the Canadian Football League. The coach of the Wildcats gave Chad a quick sales pitch: he'd play a lot, the field was wider and longer, the offense was more wide open, and the weather was nowhere near as brutal as people said. "Think it over." Chad promised he would and hung up quickly.

Sas-fucking-katchewan? He threw himself on his bed and buried his head under his pillow.

"Hey, Chad," roared Houston, "make sure you block the fooking linebacker, eh?"

"The fooking *ootside* linebacker, eh?" Black added.

The phone rang again. If anything, it was worse.

It was Vince Lombardi.

"Chad, we want you to know that if you're available in the seventh round, we're going to take you," said Lombardi.

"Oh. That's great, Coach."

"We're excited, too. Let's just hope you don't get snapped up before our turn."

"Let's hope," said Chad.

Chad slowly hung up. The last team anyone wanted to play for was the Washington Redskins under Vince Lombardi. When it came to football, there wasn't a player alive who didn't revere the legendary Lombardi. There also wasn't a player alive who hadn't heard that he was a hard-nosed, no-bullshit, uncompromising maniac who drove his players without mercy.

Lombardi or Canada? Death by torture or frostbite?

This is not turning out the way I'd hoped. . . .

'The phone.

The Dallas Cowboys. Tom Landry saying almost the exact words as Lombardi: "Chad, if you're there in round seven, we take you." The phone clicked off.

Another half hour of waiting, anticipation, and dread. And then, one last phone call.

"Hello?" said Chad, not knowing what to expect anymore but fearing the worst.

"This Chad Brown?"

"Yes."

"Chad, Chuck Noll of the Pittsburgh Steelers. We've made a trade. You're our seventh-round draft pick."

Silence.

Then birds began to sing and a rainbow spread across the sky. Life was good. Damn good.

"Chad? You there?"

"I'm here, Coach, I'm here."

"Well, say something."

"OK. Thank you. Thank you, Coach," Chad said to Chuck Noll, and he meant it with all his heart.

6
GOING PRO

Oh, no. It was happening again.

Chad couldn't believe it. It was like a recurring night-mare. They'd told him that they were only going to do it to him *once*, the first day, but they'd lied. They'd done it to him every day this week, and they showed no signs of letting up. They seemed to take joy in it, too; they liked humiliating him. He'd actually prayed last night that they would take pity on him and end this torture. But these were football players, not prone to showing mercy. They were sadists, large, brutal men who enjoyed inflicting pain on others. Especially rookies. So far, this was the worst pain he'd had to endure. They were look-ing at him now, laughing. He could feel the muscles in his throat starting to constrict. Damn. He'd thought maybe today they'd forget. He'd tried to hide. He'd whisked his tray off the line and hidden out in the far corner of the room, alone, as far away as he possibly go and still be in the room. But now massive defensive tackle Ben McGee, Chad's camp nemesis, for whom he'd become practically a personal valet, was pointing a finger at him, beckoning.

"Mr. Brown, I believe it's that time again."

Damn, Chad thought. *There it goes. My left knee. It's shaking again.* He tried to steady it by resting his hand on his kneecap. For a moment he forgot where he was. His mind was moving in circles. He had to talk to him-self to calm his nerves.

Pittsburgh Steelers training camp. 1969.

"Lunchtime serenade, rookie. Stand up on your chair and sing with pride now. And feeling. Not like yesterday."

Chad slowly pushed himself away from the table and climbed up onto his chair. Ben McGee applauded. Roy Jefferson, Terry Hanratty, and a few other veterans clinked glasses with their forks. Rookies "Mean" Joe Greene and L. C. Greenwood put their heads down and studied their plates. They knew they were next. Chad cleared his throat and began, haltingly, to sing. He had a surprisingly good voice, a clear, sweet tenor, and he had some experience; he'd sung in the Lincoln High School choir. That was different. He was part of a group. He was too embarrassed to sing a solo. And if he'd ever been forced to, the last piece he would choose would be the East Texas State fight song. Maybe if he picked up the beat, sang fast, and got it over with:

> *"Let our voices loudly ringing*
> *Echo far and near,*
> *Songs of praise the children singing,*
> *To the memory dear."*

The veterans began to bang on the table. Some clapped along. Suddenly lunchtime serenade had the feel of a revival meeting.

"Oh, yeah!" shouted Ben McGee.

"Sing it!" Jefferson pleaded.

Jesus Christ, I'm sweating, thought Chad. *I've gotta speed this up, get it over with before I have some kind of embolism.*

> *"Alma mater, alma mater,*
> *Loud her praises be.*

Hail to thee, our alma mater,
Hail, all hail, E.T."

He raced through this part and, as usual stumbled on a few of the words in the third verse, mumbling to cover his miscue. He ended the song with a tiny vocal flourish, a little reverb on that final phrase, "evermore wessing." What the hell was "wessing," anyway? He hoped that they didn't ask. He dismounted from his chair. He wished he could sink down through a trap door in the floor and disappear. He was vaguely aware of loud applause, some laughter.

"Oh, man," roared Ben McGee, "that was *beautiful!* I got tears in my eyes, I really do. In fact, you were so good"—McGee turned to the rest of the room—"I say we book him for the rest of the week. You all agree?"

More banging on tables, shouting, clinking of glasses.

Chad bit his lip. He hated this so much.

Then he sighed. At least things were going just as badly on the field.

Humiliating moment number one occurred the first day of practice during the fitness run for rookies. The object was to see how far each rookie could run in twelve minutes. The absolute bare minimum was one and a half miles. Chad, his head pounding, his chest feeling like it was going to explode, clutched his right side in pain as the offensive line coach clicked off his stopwatch. The coach shook his head.

"Didn't make the minimum, rookie. Know what that means? Sprints. After practice. Then you keep doing the run until you make it."

Chad nodded, too exhausted to speak. He'd run all out, and he'd still missed the boat. Oh, well. So he and the other rookie linemen would have do a few sprints after practice. No big deal.

Except all the other rookie linemen made the minimum. Chad ran the sprints alone. In retrospect, this was probably an omen, a sign, that *getting* to the National Football League was a lot different from *playing* in the National Football League. But that first day, sprinting after practice; his head facing down toward the University of Pittsburgh track, the red clay dirt biting his thighs, Chad still hung tightly onto his dream. Hope sprints eternal.

Every rookie was assigned to a veteran player who was supposed to show him the ropes, indoctrinate him to the policies of the Steelers. Chad was given Ben McGee, the biggest, baddest, meanest player on the team. The Steelers were in a rebuilding year. They'd only won a couple of games the year before. In the draft they'd mainly gone for defense, choosing 275-pound defensive tackle Mean Joe Greene with their first pick and, later, L. C. Greenwood, a swift defensive end. The philosophy was to shore up a porous and soft defense this year, then deal with the aging and ineffective offense next year. McGee was a throwback to a bygone era. He was tough as nails and believed in intimidation.

"You got any questions, ask me!" he thundered.

Chad nodded shyly.

"*Well?*"

"No, no questions. If I do, I'll ask."

"That's what I just *said*, didn't I?"

Chad was too intimidated even to nod. He just blinked.

"For now," McGee roared, "get my helmet and pads and bring 'em to me. And hurry up!"

Off the field, Chad served McGee his meals in the dining room, picked up his clothes at the cleaner's, and drove his car to the car wash.

On the field, McGee showed Chad no mercy, cut him no slack. McGee whaled on Chad, repeatedly blasting his nearly three hundred pounds into him, pummeling

Chad into the ground, long after the line coach blew his whistle.

Chad was stunned. He stared at McGee, his pride wounded. After all, he'd just brought Ben his favorite snacks from the grocery store and stood in line at the post office for a half hour to buy him a book of stamps.

McGee was happy to explain directly in Chad's face why he was punishing his personal valet in this ungrateful way: "This ain't East Texas State! This is the NFL, rookie!"

The days were brutal, unrelenting, filled with two-a-days in the humid Pittsburgh summer. Chad attacked each practice with total and complete determination, but as an offensive lineman he was feeling undersized and, despite four strong years at East Texas State, unprepared. Most often, Chad drew fellow rookie L. C. Greenwood in one-on-one drills. These were face-offs, two gladiators charging into each other at full speed, using every technique and weapon in their arsenal, legal or not. L.C. was simply too quick and too accomplished for him. After the whistle blew, Chad found himself pushing Greenwood in frustration. In the summer of '69, Chad wasn't having much fun.

The last week of camp Chad stood facing the inside of his locker. He stared at his clothes, stacked in neat piles. It had been a disappointing camp. Today was the day of the final cuts. He fully expected to be released. He wondered what he'd do without football.

"Coach Noll wants to see you."

The trainer said it casually and drooped his head as he darted by. *He doesn't want to look at me,* thought Chad. *Shit. I'm right. I'm out of here. I'm gone. Cut.*

He walked slowly down the corridor to Chuck Noll's office. *What could I have done differently?* he thought. He didn't know. But he was aware that this was the first time in his life that he'd lost in sports. How would he explain it to his parents, his brother, his friends back home? Chad Brown, local hero, All-American, seventh-round draft choice, gets cut by the Pittsburgh Steelers.

Noll motioned him into his office and offered him a seat.

"I'll get right to the point," he said. Chuck Noll was a straight shooter, a man who wasted no words. "We're putting you on the taxi squad, Chad. You'll practice with the team during the week, but on the weekends I want you to hook up with our semipro team. You need a little more experience, that's all. You had a good camp. We have very high hopes for you next year." Noll grinned thinly, which meant he was dismissed. Chad mumbled, "OK, thanks," and made his way out the door.

The walk back down the same corridor felt a lot shorter. Taxi squad. Semipro team on the weekends. *I'm alive,* thought Chad. *Still got my dream. I didn't make the big club. But I wasn't cut. I'm still a member of the Pittsburgh Steelers.*

Chad smiled.

At that moment, he felt as if Chuck Noll had just informed him he'd been selected to the Pro Bowl.

The Steelers suffered through a brutal 1969 season, finishing with exactly one win. They were rewarded with the number-one pick of the 1970 draft. With it, they selected strong-armed quarterback Terry Bradshaw from Louisiana Tech, touted as the team's savior. Bradshaw hit camp with a mane of golden hair, a rocket arm, and the cockiness of a gunslinger.

Chad, as well, came to camp bursting with confidence. He'd spent the off-season working out. It paid off.

He had a good camp. At one point, the coaches switched him to defense. Chad liked this experiment. He actually felt more comfortable on that side of the ball.

He preferred hitting, rather than being hit. As he survived each cut, his confidence grew. *This is going to be my year,* he thought. *The year I begin my ascent to superstardom in the NFL.*

Which was why he felt crushed when he got the call to make the long march back to Chuck Noll's office. As Chad's cleats clattered on the corridor floor, he replayed the scene from last summer: taxi squad again, semipro on the weekends. *This is getting old,* thought Chad as he opened the door to the coach's office. *Oh, well. At least I'm still a member of the Pittsburgh Steelers.*

"You've been released," said Chuck Noll.

Chad stared at him in silence. Noll's words hit him like a hammer. *"Wait a minute!"* he wanted to scream. *"You can't do this! Do you know how hard I've worked? I've been dreaming about playing in the NFL since I was nine years old."*

"Sorry," said Noll. "I wish you a lot of luck."

Thin smile. Eyes down. Meeting over.

After being cut by Pittsburgh, Chad was utterly devastated. But within twenty-four hours, he was picked up by the Houston Oilers. And Houston wanted him to play defense. He joined his new teammates Elvin Bethea, Charlie Joyner, and Dan Pastorini and played a few games immediately. He played well but once again was sent to the taxi squad. The season ended badly for Houston but on a high note for Chad. He was assured that he would be given every opportunity to win a spot on the regular roster during camp.

In Houston the next summer, Chad attacked camp with fierce abandon. He started to make a mark in preseason games. In the Hall of Fame game against the Los Angeles Rams, Chad sacked Rams quarterback Roman Gabriel twice. In another game against the New York Giants, Chad chased the elusive Fran Tarkenton out of the pocket and knocked him down, causing the ball to squirt loose. Chad dived on the ball. He recorded a sack and recovered a fumble on the same play. Routine maybe for Mean Joe Greene. Another day at the office for Bob Lily. But for Chad Brown, it was big stuff. A beginning. He was finally starting to make his presence felt as a defensive lineman.

That's why he was so crushed when Houston cut him. Damn. He couldn't play any better. He tried to analyze the Oilers' thinking. He was a little undersized, sure, but he'd played like a man possessed during the preseason. *I guess they have too many veterans at my position*, he reasoned. That was true. But Houston was no power-house. Hell, they were as bad as Pittsburgh. Now what?

A reprieve. J. D. Roberts, head coach of the New Orleans Saints, wanted to meet with him. On paper, the Saints were a troubled team. On the field, they were worse. Their only decent player was quarterback Archie Manning, an accomplished scrambler, which was a good thing because he spent every game running for his life. It didn't matter to Chad. Roberts was willing to give him a tryout. It went well and Chad was handed a contract with the Saints. The dream lived on! He had another fresh start!

The fresh start became a sour finish right after the season. Chad was once again released. At home in Dallas, glued to the couch, depressed, Chad reviewed the last few years with his brother, Ron.

"I'm not exactly tearing up the league," Chad admitted.

"Yeah, but you actually *played* in the NFL," Ron reminded him. "How many guys can say that?"

"Hundreds."

"Come on."

"I know, I know," Chad sighed. He swirled his drink, stared into his glass. "It's just that I wanted, I don't know, *more*." He looked his brother in the eye. "I think I can play in this league, I really do."

Ron's silence spoke volumes.

"OK," Chad said, finally. "Maybe that's my secret. But I need to keep trying until I get it out of my system."

Ron nodded. He understood. Then he thought for a moment. "Chad, I know a guy. Milton Grimes. I went to school with him. He's a lawyer. He became a sports agent. I think he can help you. Want me to call him for you?"

"A sports agent?"

"Give him a try."

Chad hired the agent. True to form, like most agents, he didn't call for two weeks. *What am I doing?* thought Chad. *Me, represented by an agent? It's ridiculous. I'm giving this guy 10 percent of my salary to do what? Write letters? Make phone calls? Tell people I can play football? What do I need an agent to do that for? I can do that myself. This is nuts. Agents are for superstars, movie stars, rock stars. I'm going to call him and tell him thanks, but no thanks, I'm going to be my own agent, you're fired.*

The phone rang. It was Grimes. "Chad, pack your bag. I got you a job. You're playing football again."

Chad was stunned. "I am? With who?"

"Houston."

"All right! I'm back with the Oilers!"

"Well, no. Not the Oilers. You're with the Texans."

"The who?"

"The Houston *Texans*. Of the World Football League."

"The World Football League? That's not even a *league*," said Chad, his voice rising. "It's made up of guys who are either too old, too weak, or too lousy to play in the NFL. No way I'm playing there."

"With base pay and incentives, I got you a no-cut

contract that comes to over a hundred thousand dollars."

Chad paused. A hundred grand. That was more money than he'd ever made in his life playing in the National Football League. By a *lot*.

"When do I start?"

"Tomorrow."

Smart thing getting an agent.

For every camel's back there is a straw. For Chad Brown, that straw was the World Football League.

The World Football League was created in 1974 to compete with the National Football League. In addition to the Houston Texans, the league consisted of the Birmingham Americans, Chicago Fire, Detroit Wheels, Florida Blazers, Honolulu Hawaiians, Jacksonville Sharks, Memphis Southmen, New York Stars, Southern California Sun, Portland Storm, and Philadelphia Bell. Under the headline "Standout Sports Names Return at Top in WFL," a typical program profiled team owners and such football luminaries as Louis Lee, Bruce Gelker, Rommie Loudd, and Bob Schmertz. On the Texans, Chad joined a group of aging teammates that included Sid Blanks, Garland Boyette, Al Dotson, Charlie Frazier, Willie Frazier, Mike Taliaferro, Harry Thelfiledes, Don Trull, Warren Wells, Jim Nance, and Jim Kanicki. Their photos in the program made them look at least fifty or stoned or both. The games themselves resembled old-timers' games: warm, well-meaning, soft, mushy, and played in slow motion. Chad played hard and often, though largely unnoticed. The Texans played their home games in the Astrodome in front of sparse crowds that, as the season wore on, dwindled down to a precious few—a select group of friends, family, die-hard fans with no lives and tourists with no clue.

It didn't work. Halfway through the season the team was moved to Shreveport, Louisiana (renamed the *Lou-*

isiana Texans?). Two games later the owner of the team began selling off furniture in the clubhouse and locker rooms to pay the players' salaries. Two games after that, Coach Jim Garrett, a nice, gentle man, announced the World Football League was bankrupt and the players would no longer be getting paid.

Chad sat in front of his locker, slowly unwinding the athletic tape that he had wrapped around his fingers. He stopped and studied his hands. They were large, and over the years of playing professional football they'd become battered. They'd been his only protection in the football wars, battles against the lesser foes in the small football stadium near Lincoln High, battles he'd won against double teams at East Texas State, and wars in which he'd held his own often enough against the likes of Joe Greene, L. C. Greenwood, and other stars in the National Football League. Chad examined his long, lean fingers, cracked and scarred and marred. If you saw just the hands and not the man, you might assume these fingers routinely palmed a basketball or strummed an electric guitar. A lineman's fingers are rough and chunky, oozing power, not finesse.

Chad reached his fingers out and rubbed the outside of his locker. He took a deep breath. Ron was right. Chad had accomplished what very few people had. He'd played professional football. But he knew now, for sure, that he would never become a superstar in the National Football League. That dream was over.

It was time to get another dream.

7

DO THESE STRIPES MAKE
ME LOOK FAT?

Chad looked in the mirror and stared at his reflection. He allowed his hands to move gently over his cheek, and then he rubbed his chin. Smooth. Like polished stone. Should be. This was the third time he'd shaved that day. He twisted his mouth over to the side of his face. *Whoa. Missed a spot. There's a little teeny-tiny hair sticking up there just under my right eye. Truly annoying. Maybe I should grow a beard. Then I wouldn't have to obsess over my facial hair. Nah. I'd look nasty in a beard. Tried it once. Took about a month to grow in. Came in in blotches. My face looked like that vacant dirt lot over on Macon Street. I'll just leave the mustache. Might as well whack that little hair now. But if I do that, what am I gonna do the rest of the night?*

Shit, thought Chad. *Does every athlete go through this at the end of his career? Does every jock stare at himself in the mirror and ask, "OK, Big Stuff, what now? What are you going to do with the rest of your life?" No,* Chad knew. Not every jock. If your career was long and successful and you were smart with your money, you had a lot of options. You could spend all day at the pool or on the golf course. Or, even better, you could become what every man longs to become: a consultant. But if you had merely a decent career and didn't make your fortune, you could be barely thirty years old and looking in the mirror, confused, alone, and facing a future filled not only with uncertainty but with terror. Hell, jocks are trained to *play*. When your playing days are over, what the hell are you supposed to do?

"I don't know," Chad said aloud.

He turned away from the mirror, the lone hair erectly belligerent just above his cheek. For too long—he'd lost track of exactly how long—he'd been drifting around Dallas, trying to sort it all out, trying to plan his next move. He felt stuck, frozen. He knew he had to start over, try something new. But what and where?

He recalled that his uncle had mentioned a friend or relative, Billy Lewis, who lived in Los Angeles. Maybe a change of scenery was what he needed. It would probably be good to get away from the distractions of Dallas, all his well-meaning friends and family. But mostly it would be good to escape the expectations that had been either met or missed, depending on your point of view or your state of mind. Billy Lewis. Gonna go to LA and look him up. So, with a few dollars and a few names in his pocket, Chad drove west, to Southern California, if not to find fame and fortune, to find himself.

Time drifted away, evaporated into thin air. There were weeks on friends of cousins' cots, a rash of crummy studio apartments. Finally, one day he emerged, peering into the Southern California sun, determined to build a new life. He started by making his one and only leap into coaching.

At the time, Chad was messing around with semipro ball, playing defensive end for the Los Angeles Mustangs. He'd become friends with Robert Taylor, a running back who moonlighted as an assistant coach at Southwest Community College. Taylor told him they were looking for an offensive line coach and wondered if Chad might be interested. *Coaching. Worth trying once,* Chad thought. Taylor introduced him to Lawrence

Jarmon, the athletic director. Chad was hired on the spot. It was a no-brainer for Jarmon. A former NFL lineman coaching for his community college team? It had to be a boost to the foundering program.

It wasn't. Chad was uncomfortable as a coach. He found it a challenge to communicate to the players, who demonstrated football talent ranging from minimal to none. Nothing he said would've helped anyway. The football games barely resembled athletic contests; they were more like human sacrifices. The team finished 0–10. After the season, Jarmon called the coaches into his office one by one. Chad knew he wasn't getting the key to the faculty rest room, but he wasn't expecting what he did get: advice that would turn his life around.

"I'm firing you," Jarmon announced. "Don't take it personally, I'm firing everybody."

"I don't take it personally," said Chad. "We went oh and ten and we weren't as good as our record."

"You got that right," Jarmon said.

"I don't think coaching's for me," said Chad. "I just wish I could somehow stay involved with football, though."

Jarmon sized him up. "Ever thought about officiating?"

"Officiating? I don't know. Enforcing the rules? I'm kinda used to *breaking* 'em."

Jarmon shrugged. "The LA unit is always looking for qualified people. You take the class, get certified, you'd have your stripes in no time. I think you'd be good at it."

Officiating.

Me?

Chad Brown? A zebra?

The authority on the field?

The man in stripes. The establishment. The law. The football police. Enforcer of the rules. Guardian of the game. Judge and jury. The final say. The last word.

He was liking the sound of this.

Butterflies in the pit of my stomach. Dryness in the back of my throat. It's natural, thought Chad as he maneuvered his car into a tight parking space in the lot next to the high school. *I'm working my first game, ever, as a football official. There's bound to be nerves.*

Whoo. I don't remember being this nervous playing. *Must be the newness of the thing. That's it. Plus the fact that I stick out like a sore thumb. I'm taller and bigger than all the other officials. And this uniform. Do you think these stripes make me look fat? No, those are* horizontal *stripes. These are* vertical. *Or is it the other way around? Never mind. I can't worry about my appearance right now. There are two teams on that field waiting for the officials to arrive and flip that coin.*

There had been a little more to it than he'd thought just to get to this point. Three months of classes. Game films to watch. Rule books to study. *Then took my test, got my certification. Bought my uniform. Cost me a hundred twenty dollars. Between that and my classes I'm a hundred seventy in the hole. I'm losing money on this gig. But I have a feeling it'll be worth it in the long run. It's been a blast so far and, hell, I've played the game. I know it like the back of my hand. I am psyched for this. Ready to* officially *kick some butt!*

Chad got out of his car, adjusted his black umpire's cap, and as he walked toward the field looked at the schedule in his hand.

Who's playing today? he asked himself. *Let's see. We got the Carson Colts against the Inglewood Bandits? Hmm. Never heard of them.*

One of the two other officials, balding, midforties, met him as he crossed the near sideline. He extended his hand. "Chad?"

"Yeah."

"Ev Bailey. Welcome."

"Thanks."

"Nervous?"

"Nah. Well. Maybe a little."

"You'll be fine. Really, the only thing you have to worry about is the parents."

"The . . . *parents*?"

"Oh, yeah. It's not the kids. It's the parents who'll break your balls."

Chad shifted his feet and looked right through Ev Bailey. What the hell was he talking about?

And then he saw the teams.

Twenty-two ten-year-olds swimming in their uniforms, their helmets covering their heads and faces like bowls. The biggest player on the field swatted his stomach, allowing his massive 100-pound frame to swish freely in his too-tight uniform.

"Wait a minute," Chad started to protest. "These really are *kids*."

"Sure. What'd you expect?"

"I don't know. Pop Warner. I was thinking they were high school age, junior high at least. . . ."

Ev Bailey waved at someone behind Chad. "Here comes Carlyle, our other official."

Chad swung around to see a man *older* than Ev, *limping* toward them.

"Oh, great," muttered Chad.

The Colts prepared to kick off to the Bandits. Because it was only a three-man crew, Chad was forced to cover a third of the field. He would be doing the job of both umpire and head linesman. The nerves flew away, replaced by a splitting headache.

The return kid gathered in the ball, dropped it, picked it up, and was buried under a mob of diminutive Colts. The ball skittered away. A Bandit tried to pick it up. He was tackled, hard. He started to cry. Chad whistled the play dead just as the little Bandit's parents ran onto the field. The mom soothed her son while the dad hollered at Bailey for not dropping a flag.

Carlyle limped by Chad. "The hip's acting up. I'm gonna sit this quarter out."

"Fine. Good idea," mumbled Chad.

In what seemed like a blink of an eye, he'd gone from playing in the NFL to refereeing *Rugrats*.

Chad glanced at the sky, looking for an answer, a sign, a clue. As kids shrieked and parents squawked, he knew, for his own mental health, he had to move up the officiating ladder as fast as humanly possible before he ended up in a padded little room. He instantly formulated a brand-new goal in the form of a silent prayer.

Please, Lord, let me just officiate high school.

Chad's prayer was answered within the year. In addition to working in the LA unit, he joined the South Bay unit, which covered areas south of Los Angeles, including parts of Orange County. He discovered that it was important to become friendly with each unit's assigner. Chad hung with the assigners, schmoozed with them, but mainly assured them that as long as he could get there in time, there was no game he wouldn't do. The assigners sent Chad all over the map. He quickly moved from Pop Warner to junior high school, then high school, community college, and finally college Division III. His reputation preceded him, his hard work rewarded him, his ambition fueled him. It was no sacrifice; he loved being on the field, loved being part of the game of football again. He was feeling renewed, energized. He caught the bug of the game again. It was a whirlwind of flying yellow flags, the shrill shriek of the silver whistle, long, torturous car rides through the gridlock of the city. In 1984 and 1985, a typical schedule would find Chad officiating a high school junior varsity game Thursday night in the South Bay, a varsity high school game in Los Angeles Friday night, a junior college game Saturday noon, a Division III game Saturday night, and a semipro game Sunday afternoon. Five games in four days!

For Chad, it was a crash course in officiating. He also saw it as a way to make officiating somewhat financially feasible, even at this level. A high school game paid forty-five dollars, a college game sixty dollars. Doing one a week was hardly worth the trouble. But when he did several, the money started to mount up. Adding his part-time job working the rest of the week in the Parks and Recreation Department in nearby Carson, he was beginning to make some meaningful cash. Translated, this meant he was beginning to see how officiating could go beyond being his hobby and actually become his career.

After three years of working everything from junior varsity to semipro, Chad received a letter inviting him to try out for the Big West Conference. He gathered with a group of other Division I hopefuls at the University of Southern California and worked a scrimmage with the USC football team. He knew it was rare that an official got offered a position in a major conference after only one tryout.

It was a surprise, then, when Chad got the phone call from Jack O'Cain, supervisor of officials for the Big West, offering him a job.

Chad was flying high. In four short years he'd gone from baby-sitting ten-year-olds in a sandlot in Inglewood to officiating a shootout between Fresno State and New Mexico State. He felt he was riding a rocket ship, careerwise, and he considered himself lucky. He'd also taken a major step personally.

In early 1984, while working at his job in the Parks and Recreation Department, he looked up from his desk one day and found himself staring at a vision who'd just walked in the door. She was an absolute knockout. Then she opened her mouth. He was even more floored. She spoke with an authority and wisdom that he'd never before encountered. The woman breezed out of the office as dramatically as she'd come in. Chad never heard her name. But he knew he had to find that out and more.

Her name was Deborah Jones, and after two years of an intense and beautiful courtship they were married in the summer of 1986. As Chad began his first season in the Big West, he contemplated all the events of the past few years and saw how swiftly his life had changed, especially now that he was married and planning a family.

In the back of his mind there was another thought as well. Chad knew he wouldn't be satisfied stopping here, being a major college umpire. The bug he'd caught when he began officiating a few years earlier had become a fever. He wanted it all. He wanted to reach for the stars. He wanted the National Football League.

Chad decided to begin the application process. The idea came from Joe Kozak, one of the other umpires in the Big West. A fatherly type, though not much older than Chad, Kozak encouraged Chad to get the ball rolling. He was convinced that out of all the officials in the conference, Chad had the best shot to get to the Show.

"You've got a helluva future, Chad, anyone can see that. You're strong at your position and you're a former player. They like that."

The process was a piece of cake. All Chad had to do was write a letter to the National Football League, expressing interest in becoming an official. The league responded with a form letter asking for a birth certificate, a written application, and a conference schedule. The

NFL informed Chad that the league would be sending one or more former officials to scout a couple of his games. Simple enough.

Except that what followed was the kind of cloak-and-dagger secrecy usually reserved for spy novels. It was almost as if Chad were applying for a position in the CIA rather than the NFL. To begin with, the league wouldn't identify who the scouts were and when they were coming.

"That makes sense," Chad reasoned. "Don't want to get me nervous, throw me off my game. So I'll just forget about it and go about my business. Doesn't matter who's watching me. Doesn't matter at all."

But walking the field before each game, Chad would wonder whether this was the one. *Is today the day? Are there NFL scouts here, checking me out?* He'd scan the stands, looking for likely suspects. In Vegas, in the midst of a September heat wave, he spotted two guys sitting near the fifty who stood out like sore thumbs. *Yeah. Talk about obvious. Look at them. It's Vegas, in the middle of the desert, about a hundred and fifty degrees on the field, and these guys are wearing* suits.

Ah, damn. They could be scouts, they could be touts, they could be from New Jersey, they could be cold-blooded. What am I doing? This is crazy. Gotta just concentrate on my game and not give a rat's ass if some-one's here from the NFL. Probably all hype, anyway. I mean, they're not really interested in me. Think about it. Is the NFL really gonna send somebody from New York City to watch Chad Brown umpire a game between these two football powers, UNLV and San Jose State?

Apparently so.

A month later Chad received a certified letter inform-ing him that he had been selected as a "candidate" for the National Football League. He was to report to Jack O'Cain's office and meet with a supervisor from the league. Stunned but delighted, Chad reported to O'Cain's office expecting a laid-back, informal interview. Instead, the NFL supervisor interrogated him for two grueling hours, then gave him a one-hour written intelligence and psychological test. Chad staggered out of O'Cain's office feeling as if he'd been grilled like a hamburger. He was slightly surprised when the National Football League called to inform him that he was now a "finalist." On to the next phase: the infamous background check.

Chad was told that the league now would examine each finalist *thoroughly,* as if so far the process had been blasé. An NFL representative from the league office promised that they would now dig deep into Chad's past. He explained it to Chad this way: "We call current employers, past employers, friends, relatives, we do a detailed financial history, interview neighbors, and do an extensive educational history. We will often interview a former teacher. In your case, we've decided to interview your second-grade teacher."

Chad said nothing. He couldn't remember if anything significant had occurred during second grade. He wasn't too concerned, since his second-grade teacher had been dead for years. *These guys are so thorough, they'll probably still want to interview her,* Chad thought.

One late March morning in 1990, Chad was at work and Deborah was at home with their three-month-old twins, Devin and Trent. The doorbell rang. Deborah saw a smartly dressed man in his fifties wearing a sport coat and tie waiting outside. She opened the door. The man smiled graciously.

"Good morning. I'm a private investigator hired by the National Football League. I'm here to do a background check on your neighbor Chad Brown."

Thrown, Deborah nodded slightly. "Uh-huh."

The investigator continued. "I wonder if I could ask

you some questions about Mr. Brown. Nothing too personal. You know, what is he like as a neighbor? Is he pleasant, courteous, respectful of your property? Does he yell at his kids? Does he take care of his trash? Lotta people coming and going over there? Lotta loud, wild parties? That sort of thing. And don't worry, anything you say will be held in the strictest confidence."

Deborah paused. She was sitting pretty here. Of course, she knew she had to tell him the truth. It was only a matter of time before he figured it out himself. Plus, Deborah couldn't lie. But she could have a little fun.

"Before we start, there's something important I think you should know about Chad," Deborah said.

The investigator flipped open a leather notebook and produced an expensive ballpoint pen. *Wow. This is great. Brown's neighbor has a juicy story to tell. To be honest, the neighbors are usually useless. Unless they are nosy or crazy or the candidate has a bunch of bodies buried in his toolshed, which isn't that often.*

"Now, what's this important thing you want to tell me about Chad Brown?" the investigator asked, pen at the ready.

"Well, it's very important that you know that I'm not his neighbor, I'm his wife."

"His wife lives next door?" he blurted out, confused.

"No," Deborah replied patiently. "You came to the wrong house."

The investigator nodded and clicked his pen shut. "Well. This is embarrassing. It was very nice talking to you, Mrs. Brown."

"Likewise."

He waved awkwardly, then headed quickly over to the *neighbor*'s front door.

Amazing, she said to herself. *How did he get the*

*wrong house? We get mail from the NFL. I know they
have our address.*

"One thing's for sure," she said aloud. "If I ever need
a private investigator, I won't be hiring him."

It all came down to this.

The interview.

Chad sat in a conference room at a large circular table, polished so well you could almost shave in it. Oak?
Teak? Walnut? He rubbed his palm over the finish, trying to guess the grain of wood. It calmed his nerves
momentarily. Then he heard voices calling his name. He
leaped to his feet as four men, faces familiar to him from
TV, entered the room. Rows of flashing teeth. Hands
extended and gripped in greeting. "Sit down, Chad," one
said, the most familiar, the one in charge. Chairs scraping. A deep breath. This was the hardest part. By far.
He was in the dark, too, flying blind. Nobody had
prepped him. He had no idea what to expect. Their
names came. He knew them all, legendary referees: Art
McNally, Ron DeSouza, Jack Reader, and the man running the show, the director of NFL officiating, Jerry Seeman. Small talk first. How was your flight? Hotel OK?
First time in New York? Sorry for the lengthy and ex-
haustive application process. Contrary to what the public
thinks, we don't choose just *anyone* to be an official in
the National Football League. They seemed genuinely
nice, truly interested in him, sincere in making this work.
Until Seeman asked one question that cut the room like
a laser.

"So, Chad, other than umpire, what other positions do
you work?"

"Well, to tell you the truth, Jerry, none. I'm an umpire. That's my only position."

Dead silence. Chad absently polished the tabletop
again. The clink of a glass. Clearing of someone's throat.

The silence couldn't have lasted more than a few seconds, but it felt like a decade.

But it's the truth, damn it. I am an umpire. I've worked years to succeed in the middle. Didn't they scout me at this position? Isn't that why I'm here?

"To be honest with you, Chad," Jerry said evenly, "we got other guys on the list who've worked other spots. They're a little more versatile. See, our policy is to bring in officials who'll work the flanks, *then* we move them into the middle. That's the way we like to do it. Been our policy for years."

Clink. Clink. Ahem.

These tiny noises were giving Chad a giant headache. *I'm not blowing this, am I?* he worried. *I can't blow this.*

The conversation turned. Twenty questions later, amid too-loud laughter, Chad found himself on a tour of the facility. More meeting rooms. An up-to-the-minute tape and film facility where Seeman viewed game films and created weekly training tapes. Very posh. Very impressive. Then, finally, an exit interview alone with Seeman. *I've got to say something here,* thought Chad. *Clarify. Salvage this trip.*

"Jerry," Chad said, "I don't have a problem working any other position. But my primary position, the position I prefer to work, is umpire. I am an umpire," Chad added for emphasis, and as he shook Jerry's hand good-bye and headed for the elevator, he knew that in his attempt to straighten everything out he'd just screwed everything up.

"For those of you on the right side of the plane," the pilot droned, "feast your eyes on a magnificent view of the Grand Canyon. For those of you on the left—"

Sure. That's where I'm sitting, Chad said to himself.

"—look at the vast wasteland below."

No, Chad, that's not miles of barren desert; that's *your life. . . .*

"Sir, would you care for the prime rib or lobster Newburg?"

Chad blinked his eyes open. He must've dozed off. He sat up and ordered the prime rib. Might as well pamper himself. Damn. He could get used to first class. The NFL officials always flew first class. Too bad this time in first class would be his last time.

He shook his head. *Man, did I blow it. Sure, Art McNally said something about being guaranteed a spot in the World League, but what's that? Doing games in Poland or Finland or some other European football hotbed? God, I want the NFL so badly. So badly I can taste it.* But right now the taste in his mouth was a combination of airplane prime rib and bitter disappointment.

"For those of you on the right side of the plane, admire the natural splendor of Yosemite National Park. And for those of you on the left side—"

"That's me," Chad said aloud, fully awake.

"—look at the wreckage down below."

At first Chad didn't have the heart to tell Deborah the whole truth.

"It went well, Deb. Really well. You should see the film facility they have—"

"How'd the interview go?"

"Then they took me on a tour of the whole place—"

"Chad, tell me about the *interview*."

"Oh yeah. The interview. With Seeman."

Chad smiled, then sank into his favorite overstuffed chair. The smile sank along with him.

"I blew it. I guess I didn't know what to expect. They offered me the World League."

"The World League. Well. That's . . . something."

"That it is."

Deborah smiled at her husband, then touched his hand. "I'm proud of you, Chad. The NFL flew you to New York as a potential official. That's a real accomplishment. Not many guys get this far."

Not many guys get to play in the National Football League. Not many guys get to officiate in the World League. He was getting sick of coming so damn *close*.

For the next month or so Chad fell into a slump. It was March, the off-season. His day job now was working in the Recreation Department at UCLA. Normally even-keeled, he found himself on edge. He even snapped at Dion Veloz, one of the kids who worked for him, his officemate and right-hand man, for no reason. As April approached, Chad started to reconcile himself to a season in the World League. It would be good experience. He'd checked it out and was told it was a training ground for the NFL. Three, four years working there and he might get another shot. *Tell you what, though,* Chad swore to himself. *If I have another interview with Seeman, I'll tell him I'll drive the bus if he wants me to. Jesus Christ. I had my shot. How could I have been so* dumb?

The phone rang. *Probably that guy from the American Kennel Club calling to book the soccer field for their upcoming dog show. I lead an exciting life, you know that?*

"Chad," he said into the phone. It was his standard greeting. "Hello" didn't identify him. Saying his name saved a step.

"Chad Brown?"

The voice was familiar, but Chad couldn't place it. "Yes?"

"This is Jerry Seeman."

Seeman paused dramatically while Chad held his breath.

"Chad . . ."

Seeman paused again, and then he spoke the six words that would change Chad Brown's life forever.

"Welcome to the National Football League."

HALFTIME
IV

8
BUBBA

Ty Detmer tries two passes and overthrows Jerry Rice and Terrell Owens. Detmer shakes his head. Three and out for the Niners. They head off the field. As Kevin Gogan walks by Chad, he says, "No shit, Chad, we have to talk."

Midway through the first quarter, Carolina lines up for a fifty-two-yard field goal. This time John Kasay keeps his eyes on the ground, refusing to acknowledge anyone. Gritting his teeth, he charges into the ball left-footed and booms a torpedo shot through the uprights with ten yards to spare. He pumps his arm like a hockey player scoring a goal. The shocked crowd murmurs. Carolina's ahead, 3–0.

The first quarter ends with the score 3–0 and Detmer looking ill. Chad replaces a divot with his foot as Kevin Gogan approaches, holding his helmet by its strap. Gogan sports a Marine buzz cut and has a face that looks like a dance floor. At six feet, seven inches he's one of the few NFL players who can look Chad Brown in the eye.

"Chad."

"How you doing, Kevin?"

"How'm I doin'? I just got through paying fourteen thousand dollars in fines because of you. That's how I'm doing. You got it in for me."

At the beginning of the season, *Sports Illustrated*

named Kevin Gogan the dirtiest player in the National Football League. Gogan actually likes the reputation but likes his money more.

"We don't have it in for you, man."

"Then explain those fines."

"It's chop blocks. They're gettin' you for chop blocks."

"Chop blocks," Gogan sneers. "You need a *partner* for a chop block. You need someone to go low. I don't have a partner in this league. I'm a lone wolf, you know that. And with my size, I ain't goin' low."

"What do you want me to do?"

"I want you to split the fines with me."

Chad breaks up. "Excuse me. I got a game to officiate." He starts to walk away.

Gogan chases him. "I don't mean fifty-fifty. We can go sixty-forty."

Chad laughs. "Man, you are crazy."

"Seventy-thirty? Come on! It's an investment!"

The second quarter is all Carolina. Two more field goals, then a sustained drive down the field. The offense is smart and varied. Fred Lane carries the bulk of the running load, and Beuerlein mixes up his passes—sprint outs, slants, dump-offs. On a second-down play, midway through the quarter, Beuerlein hands the football to William Floyd, who rams right into Ken Norton, then wriggles loose for another couple of yards.

Floyd leaps up, tosses the ball back at Chad, and screams at Norton, "You can't tackle me, man! You can't tackle me!"

Norton shoves Floyd and shouts back, "Don't bring that shit in here! I'm telling you, bitch, don't bring it in here!"

Chad, as calmly as talking to his ten-year-old twin boys, says, "Now, we don't need to hear that."

Fred Lane leads Floyd away, and Lee Woodall puts an arm around Norton.

On the next play, Beuerlein throws a strike to Rocket over the middle. He streaks past Marquez Pope and Darnell Walker and curls into the end zone. Touchdown. Kasay kicks the point after, and Carolina leads the 49ers 16–0.

During the TV time-out, Gogan jogs over to Chad as he takes a hit from a water bottle.

"You believe this shit?"

"Well, your number one's not playing . . . ," Chad says, referring to Steve Young.

"Not *that* shit," Gogan says. "Kevin Greene's got his hand up in my face this whole half and you're looking away."

"Really?" Chad acts surprised. He knows Gogan's working him. "I'll have to watch that, Goge."

"Thanks. Because I don't wanna have to get dirty."

Toward the end of the half, the 49ers finally muster a drive. Detmer lobs a pass to Terrell Owens, who finds another gear as he runs under the ball. The Carolina defender, Doug Evans, slips in the soggy grass and goes down. Owens waltzes into the end zone untouched. The crowd's been waiting for a play like this. They roar.

For Owens, it's time for his touchdown dance. It's a classic. He stands ramrod straight and pretends to flick imaginary pieces of lint off his uniform. Then he races full speed toward the sideline.

Gogan, on his way to the bench, passes Chad. He nods toward Owens. "What the hell was that?"

"I have no clue."

Gogan shrugs. "Really? I thought you knew everything."

The half ends with Carolina up 16–7. It's a total role reversal. The Panthers are prepared and pumped up while the 49ers seem tentative and out of sync.

\voy of security guards escorts the officials off the field and leads them under a maze of metal girders beneath Three Com Stadium. Chad cuts down a narrow concrete passageway and goes into the officials' locker room.

Closet is more like it.

And a shitty closet at that.

There is a battered couch, a couple of folding chairs, a black-and-white Sony circa 1983, a battered minifridge stocked with generic soda and questionable cheese, a toilet in the corner separated only by the back of the couch, and, hidden against the wall, a stall shower. No one cares about the accommodations. They're used to it and there's no time to complain. The seven officials have twelve minutes to fill out foul cards, sheets listing all the infractions called in the first half.

Chad pencils in his card. He dropped two flags in the half. Both were blatant fouls. No doubt about them. He *saw* them both, never anticipated either one. That was the key. You can't *assume* it; you have to *see* it. That was one of the first lessons taught to him by Jerry Markbreit, his first and only referee until this year, when Chad was moved to Hochuli's crew. He smiles, thinking of Jerry. Markbreit was his mentor, his roommate, his friend.

Seven years as an umpire in the National Football League. Seven years and his eye on the Super Bowl.

Chad lets out a wisp of air.

Seven years ago, when he was a rookie, he didn't think he'd last the season. . . .

Sam Huff, Jim Brown, Johnny Unitas, Walter Payton, Deacon Jones, Lawrence Taylor, Joe Montana, John Elway.

Jim Tunney, Norm Schachter, Art McNally, Tommy Bell, Red Cashion.

Legends of the Game.

Add to the list Jerry Markbreit.

Four Super Bowls, twenty-two years in the National Football League, possessor of a keen wit and an encyclopedic knowledge of the rules. The *Man* in the league. A true superstar.

And Chad Brown's first NFL crew chief.

Chad was numb with nervousness.

No reason to be, Chad tried to convince himself. *I'm ready. Couldn't be more ready. I've gone over and over the rule book, studied it until all the sentences started to meld together and lose their meaning. I've watched game tapes until I was bleary-eyed. I've sat through hours and hours of training clinics. I worked on my mechanics in scrimmages and worked out every day so I'd look trim and fit in my uniform. I spent April through June in Europe officiating in the World League, doing two games a week. I am so ready.*

So why the hell am I so nervous?

Two reasons: fear of the unknown and severe performance anxiety.

Simply put, what if Jerry and I don't get along and what if I screw up?

OK, now that I've cleared that up, let's get this over with and meet the Man, thought Chad.

He scanned the banquet room in the hotel, looking for Jerry and the rest of his crew. Jerry saw him first. He stood, waved at Chad, and grinned, and Chad made his way toward the empty seat Jerry had reserved right next to him at the crew's table.

Chad's first surprise was Jerry's size. The Man couldn't be more than five-ten, maybe even five-nine. Chad was tempted to say, "Nice to meet you, Jerry. Wow. You look a lot bigger on TV." First thing out of his mouth, probably wouldn't go over so well.

Actually, this was not the first time they'd met.

They'd spoken briefly on the phone. Markbreit had called a few weeks ago with the news that Chad had been placed on his crew in the umpire spot. Jerry had called to welcome Chad and to tell him how genuinely excited he was to include him as a member of what he claimed was the number-one crew in the league.

"Chad, you're going to learn a lot and you're going to have a lot of fun," Jerry promised.

"I'm looking forward to it, I really am. It's an honor to be on your crew, Jerry."

"Well, we have a name, Chad. They call us the A team."

"The A team. I like that."

"Oh." Markbreit paused as if he'd just remembered something else to tell Chad and wasn't quite sure how to say it. "There's a guy on our crew, Tom Sifferman. The back judge. Nice guy. Funny guy. Keeps us all loose."

"Yeah?" Chad was anticipating now. He knew something strange was coming.

"Sif gave you a nickname."

"Uh-oh."

"Yeah. Starting right now, you will no longer be called Chad. From now on, your name is . . ."

"*Bubba!*" Jerry called as he pumped Chad's hand in the banquet room. "Great to finally meet you face-to-face. Or, I should say, face-to-the-top-of-my-head."

The crew laughed as Jerry steered Chad to the empty seat next to him. "Guys, meet our new umpire . . . Bubba Brown!"

Laughs and handshakes all around. "Hope you don't mind the nickname," Sifferman said. "It's after Bubba Smith."

"As opposed to after *mine bubba*, which is Yiddish for '*my grandmother*,' " explained Markbreit.

More laughter.

It was overwhelming. The laughter, the camaraderie, the confidence exuded by these men. Chad felt truly privileged to have been invited into their fraternity.

"Bubba, huh?" He scowled at Sifferman for a nanosecond, then dropped that visage and switched on a wide welcoming grin of his own. "I'll try it on. See if it fits."

Scraping of chairs on the wood floor. Spoons clattering congratulations against glass. Soul slaps all around.

Chad was *in*.

9
NOT FOR LONG

Where you going, Chad?"

"Just down the hall."

"Bathroom again?"

"Yeah." Then, quickly, "Must've had too much coffee."

Markbreit, Sifferman, and the rest of the crew all nod sympathetically. They all knew the real reason Chad is hitting the head for the hundredth time in the last hour. They've all gone through it themselves.

First-game jitters. Flop sweat. The shakes. Your first NFL game is five minutes away, and you're in and out of the bathroom working the Bladder Bowl. This is a day you'll never forget. Every NFL official can tell you every last detail of his first game.

Chad Brown. August 5, 1992. The Buffalo Bills at the Minnesota Vikings. A meaningless preseason game to most people. To Chad, the most important game of his life.

Chad comes out of the bathroom, casually clicks his ballpoint pen, then fumbles his game card. It flutters to the floor.

Markbreit picks it up, hands it to Chad, and smiles. "You OK?" The words are phrased as a question but voiced as a concern.

"Yeah. I'm good. I'm *excited*. I mean, just a few months ago I was in the Big West Conference. Now I'm doing my first NFL game. It's unbelievable. Man, what the hell was in that *coffee*?"

He spins, drops his pen, picks it up, darts into the bathroom.

Markbreit and Sifferman share a sympathetic look.

"For crissakes," says Sifferman, "let's get the damn game started before he backs up the toilet."

Finally Chad is on the field. The national anthem rises, falls, ends. More than sixty thousand fans, far too many of them shirtless and wearing that ridiculous Viking helmet, are on their feet stomping, whooping, awaiting the opening kickoff that signifies not only the start of the game but also the dawning of hope itself: *This could be our year. This could be the year we'll make the play-offs, win the championship, and appear in the Super Bowl.* This hope is mirrored miraculously at this exact moment across the country in stadiums in Green Bay and Dallas and Tampa and San Diego. But here, in the Twin Cities, the Vikings' worshipers are gone, out of their minds, lost in an irrational *frenzy* that makes them seem to Chad like an angry mob, making him desperately, once again, for what seems like, conservatively, the ten thousandth time, want to piss.

This need is forgotten as the football is sideswiped by the Vikes' soccer-style kicker and boomed end over end like a cannon shot toward the goal line. The need is replaced by Jerry Markbreit's voice, a soothing voice that last night, as they shared a room in the hotel, tried gently to prepare him for this very moment.

"I know you're going to be anxious, but just try to relax out there. That's the main thing. Take things slow. And make sure you see the whole foul, the complete violation, the whole thing. *Then* throw your flag."

Chad took this in. He considered writing the advice down but thought Jerry's words might stay more securely implanted in his mind if he simply repeated them aloud, in his own words.

"So don't anticipate. See the penalty first."

"Exactly." Markbreit looked pleased. This was a role he enjoyed—football professor. It was especially rewarding because he could see by Chad's eyes that he was getting through to his prized student. "Remember, Chad, a slow flag is acceptable in the league. Don't be in a hurry to throw your flag. *See* it. Be *sure* you see it."

Chad sees it. He definitely sees it. It's almost as if there's a halo of light around it. The arm reaches out and then up, way up, an obvious grab, and, incredibly, right smack in front of him, an even more obvious takedown. It's so blatant it almost looks fake, like a takedown in professional wrestling. *Damn*, thinks Chad, *my first flag on the first play in my first NFL game. And it's as obvious as the nose on my face. It can't get any better than this. Thank you, Lord, for making my first one so* easy.

The hand to the belt. Fingers gripped tightly around the yellow flag. *Don't want to drop the damn thing. Want to send it up, up, up, not too high—that'd look arrogant—but not too low and wimpy, either; that'd look like some weak rookie shit. There it goes! Sailing in a nice arc, above helmet-level where everyone can see it, plop, thud, perfect landing, too. And I saw that foul! No doubt about it!*

Whistle blowing the play dead. The pile of bodies tangled over, under, and on top of one another, pretzeled together as if this were a game of Twister played among giants. Chad, legs churning, chews up the distance between him and Markbreit. He didn't expect this so soon. No one did. Chad's calm, even stoic, exterior betrays a Roberto Benigni–like celebration going on inside him. Markbreit waits, eagerly, to announce to the immediate world, over his portable microphone, Chad Brown's first NFL foul.

Then the scene slows down. Goes to super super slow motion. The picture becomes fuzzy; the players shift weirdly out of focus. Everything's messed up. Whacked out. Confused. Jerry's mouth opens as wide as a cavern, and his voice comes out distorted, at the wrong speed, as he asks simply:

"What did you see, Chad?"

"Huh?"

"What did you *see*?"

"I think I got a holding call, Jerry, a takedown."

"You *think*?"

"No, no. I do. I know I do. I *saw* it."

"OK, good. Who's it on? What's the number?"

"Well, that's the thing, Jerry. . . ."

"What?"

"I forgot."

"You forgot the number?"

"No, actually, Jerry, I forgot which, uh, team."

"*What?*"

"I know. It's kind of embarrassing."

"Chad."

"Yeah, Jerry?"

"Think about it."

Jerry waits. Chad looks at him blankly.

"You got two choices," Jerry says helpfully.

"I know. Minnesota or Buffalo."

"Good. Very good."

"Had to be kicking or receiving."

"That's right. It was a kickoff."

"Wait, I think it was receiving. No, no, hold it, *kicking*. That's right. Kicking. Definitely."

"You sure?"

Chad looks miserably at Markbreit. "Jerry . . . I . . . forgot."

A sigh from Markbreit loud enough in Chad's mind to quiet the crowd.

"Pick up the flag," Marbreit says finally in a whisper.

"Yeah, right," says Chad, moving as fast he can. Damn. Maybe no one saw it. Markbreit scurries toward the line of scrimmage as if nothing had happened. Chad swoops up his flag, stuffs it into his pocket, and dashes alongside Markbreit.

"Next time I'll remember the number."

"I'll be happy if you remember the goddamn *team*."

Weirdly enough, the call frees Chad from anxiety for the rest of the game. After all, what can happen now that can possibly be *worse*? By the second half, the Vikings and Bills are showcasing players who are trying to make the roster. The pressure is off. In the official's definition, the remainder of the game is perfect, meaning it is completely uneventful.

After the game, Markbreit gathers his crew in the officials' locker room.

"Good game, everybody. I was very happy to see how well you worked together. And, Bubba, except for that one slight memory lapse, when you suddenly came down with amnesia, you did a fine job."

"For a rookie," snorts Sifferman.

Jerry glares at him.

"Hey, I'm trying to razz him."

Markbreit reaches behind him and hands Chad a football and a program of the game. On them, each member of the crew has signed his name.

"It's a tradition after your first game to receive a ball and game program signed by your crew. The 'X' is Sifferman. You are now officially one of us. Congratulations, Chad."

"Thank you," Chad says softly.

It was odd, but after just one game Chad felt as if he *did* belong and that he had officiated a strong game. As if to prove the point, during the week, after viewing the game film in New York, Jerry Seeman called Markbreit to praise the work of the crew in general and Chad, the rookie umpire, in particular.

"Got a question, though," Seeman said. "Chad made a great call on that takedown during the opening kickoff. Why the hell did you pick up his flag, Jerry?"

"Let's play word association."

"I'm game," says Chad.

"Rookie."

"Nervous."

"Roommate."

"Markbreit."

"*Markbreit.*"

"Mentor. No, friend. *Father.*"

"Sifferman."

"Funny."

"Umpire."

"Bubba."

"Chad."

"Nervous."

"First regular-season game."

"Scared. Make that scared witless."

He leans back in his chair and cups his hands behind his head. He's through with *this* game. He studies the visitor across his desk. Takes a moment. Then speaks slowly, that South Dallas twang poking its way in every once in a while. . . .

"Lemme tell you a story about my first year in the National Football League. Give you an idea of what I went through.

"We're in Atlanta. Falcons playing somebody, don't remember who, doesn't matter. Early in the season, maybe the third or fourth game. During pregame, I have my ritual, a whole list of things I gotta do. Lotta people think the officials are dropped on the field by a helicopter five minutes before the game starts. That's not the way it goes. We have a whole lot of preparation, a lot of things we have to do before the kickoff.

"Anyway, I was coming out of the Atlanta locker room, heading back onto the field. I had just finished filling out my uniform violations card. There was a problem with Deion Sanders, who was playing for the Falcons at the time. He was wearing an illegal headband that stuck out of his helmet. It said 'Nike' on it. Deion had received several letters from the league telling him he couldn't wear that headband.

"I said to him, 'Deion, if you don't adjust your headband, pop it inside your helmet, the league's going to fine you. Gonna fine you big-time.'

"Deion said, 'Fine me. I don't care. I don't care how much, either. Nike's gonna pay the fine.'

"So I'm leaving the locker room and I'm walking toward Jerry Glanville, who was the head coach of Atlanta at the time. He's standing there, arms folded, kind of looking me over. He didn't look so happy. I guess he was thinking, *Got me a rookie umpire to deal with. I wonder if he knows what he's doing.*

"He stops me.

" 'You new in the league?' he says.

" 'Yeah. I'm Chad Brown. I'm the umpire.'

" 'Chad Brown, huh? You know what NFL stands for?'

" 'No.'

" '*Not For Long.*'

"Later, I found out that my crew had set this up with Glanville, but at the moment he said that to me, I was devastated. I was having a pretty rough adjustment from the college game to the pro game, and this sure didn't help."

"Word association, one more time.

"First regular-season game ever."

"*Fear*. Blinding fear."

Just my luck, thought Chad. *My first game as an NFL umpire in the regular season and I'm on* Monday Night Football. *Couldn't be more visible. Here I am, getting ready to police the Super Bowl champion Washington Redskins and their arch rivals, the Dallas Cowboys, two of the best in the business, and two teams who actually despise each other. That's me, standing on the fifty-yard line in JFK Stadium, in front of sixty-five thousand maniacs in the stands and another bazzillion viewers watching on television, including my family, friends, and all the other players and officials in the National Football League. And since I'm standing in the middle of the line of scrimmage before every play and I'm a large black man in vertical zebra stripes, I'm rather hard to miss. Great way to start your career, Chad. Right smack in front of the whole football world.*

"You'll be fine," Markbreit said last night in the room.

"No. *You'll* be fine," said Chad. "You've done this a few times before. I haven't."

"Look, there's a first time for everything, right? You'll get through this. Believe me, I was just as nervous as you are before my first game, if it makes you feel any better."

"It doesn't."

My luck again, Chad thought. *I draw last year's Super Bowl referee and a freaking living legend. Why couldn't I have drawn some other schmuck? Jesus, listen to me. I've been rooming with Jerry so much during the preseason, I'm starting to think in Yiddish.*

"It's not like you've never done this before, Bubba. You've officiated a few football games in your life. It's just like college. Except different."

Yeah. A lot different, thought Chad as the Redskins collided with the Cowboys in the first play of the game. *Way different*. As the game went on, and throughout that first season, Chad identified three major differences between the college and pro game.

First, there was the *intensity*. A typical NFL game is played with approximately the same fervor as a bowl game. It doesn't even matter who is playing. It could be Minnesota–Denver or Carolina–Chicago. For whatever reason—the high level of competition, the one-on-one combat, the lure of fame and fortune, the agony of losing, the fear of injury, or the terror of being released— the players in the National Football League play *high*. Linemen, in particular. They arrive in the meat grinder beyond rage and for the whole game remain in a virtual lather.

The second difference Chad saw immediately was the extraordinary *athleticism* of the players. NFL players are truly the best athletes in the universe. The college game presented much more variation. In the Big West Conference, Chad often saw excellent athletes lined up next to blobs with pro-sized bulk but no skill. In the National Football League, everyone is good. No. That's not true. Everyone is *great*. Even human edifices, buildings with heads, such as Gilbert Brown and Jerry Ball, are amazingly athletic. As massive as they are, they can *move*.

The third difference, the most obvious, was the *speed*. Every player in the National Football League, including the 350-pound denizens of the meat grinder, is fast. Very fast. The game itself, therefore, is built on speed. Chad was expecting this. He knew he had to adjust to the speed differential between the college and pro game. He was totally taken by surprise by something else: the difference in speed between preseason and the regular season. Markbreit reminded him of this often. He warned Chad that, during exhibition games, the players operate at three-quarters speed, even half-speed. They turn it up, all the way up, during the regular season. Chad couldn't envision *faster* players. He tried to crank up the game in his mind. It was pointless. It's impossible to *imagine* speed. But here it was. The regular season. The marginal players were gone, replaced by nothing but meteors. Blurs at every position. The slower players who were in training camp during the summer were now either playing in Europe or looking for another line of work. That Monday night game, Chad spent most of the first quarter frozen in his umpire's stance, a statue, an observer of the action around him, barely a participant in the game. He felt as if he were watching a videotape of a football game on fast-forward.

Standing rigidly at midfield during a TV time-out, Chad scratched something in pencil onto his game card as Jerry approached. He placed a gentle hand on the umpire's shoulder.

"How you doin', Bubba?"

"Hangin' in there. I'm feeling things out, I guess. You were right, Jerry. They're so *fast*."

"You'll adjust. You're going to be a great umpire in this league, kid."

Chad stuffed his game card into his pocket. "Well, maybe. But not today."

Chad trotted back toward the middle. He fiddled with his whistle, took a deep breath. He had worked out over the summer with Gordie Wells, one of the best umpires ever to work the position. Gordie had given Chad insight and knowledge, a hundred pointers, things to look for and look out for. The problem was, everything Gordie had taught him had momentarily flown right out of his head and was fluttering through the air now like a million penalty flags.

Actually, it's good that I'm having this kind of game,

Chad said to himself, *because there's nowhere to go from here but up.*

It wasn't a very fast ascent.

Depending on who was within earshot, Chad would refer to his first year in the National Football League as either an important learning experience or one rough adjustment. Either way, that rookie season almost every aspect of his new life in the National Football League was a struggle.

To begin with, it was difficult to deal with the travel. Weekends had been downtime, family time. He always looked forward to kicking back with Deborah and the twins, who were now three years old. It wasn't easy packing up every Saturday and leaving Deborah home alone with them. Chad also wrestled with the enormous amount of study and paperwork that was heaped on him every week. There were weekly open-book exams on specific rules and game situations. Once he arrived in the city where the game was being played that week, he met with his crew for a lengthy—several hours at least—pregame meeting. They went over their exams and reviewed a weekly training tape, a forty-five-minute video of good calls, blown calls, missed calls, unusual calls, and controversial calls compiled and narrated by Jerry Seeman. This was *before* every game, before Chad even slipped on his uniform.

There was even more to learn on the field. Perhaps the biggest single adjustment for Chad involved his greatest gift, his vision. According to the well-worn cliché ("You're *blind*, Ump!"), most officials can't *see.* During the play-offs and Super Bowl, one of the most popular and funniest television commercials showed a football referee in a doctor's office taking, and failing, an eye exam. In the National Football League, what you see depends on where you look. Somewhere during the second half of his first game, Chad discovered that he was looking in the wrong place. All habits are hard to break, and this one was a bitch. He was used to watching the ball. He now had to force himself to keep his eyes out of the backfield, *off* the quarterback, *away* from the football. *Remember,* he kept reminding himself before and during each game, *concentrate only on the meat grinder. Your eyes should just be on the guys who are your responsibility—the two guards and the center. Don't let your eyes wander! There they go; they're wandering! Bring 'em back to the grinder!* At some point, he had developed official's astigmatism. If he were a racehorse, he would've been fitted with blinders. Hell, officiating in college, he could look where he wanted. No problem. The game was slower; he could follow the ball *and* the action right here in the heart of the meat grinder and not lose sight of anything that wasn't kosher happening in combat. Fouls rarely got by him. In the National Football League, so far, Chad hadn't even *seen* a foul. He had, however, *called* one.

Fairly certain he'd seen a takedown, he'd thrown his flag late in the Redskins–Cowboys game, his first regular-season violation ever. This time Chad remembered both the player's number and the team he was on. Unfortunately, it was a phantom foul, there one second in front of him, then, *poof*, gone in a cloud of smoke and a sea of arms. The penalty made a second appearance later in the week in Seeman's training tape as a blown call.

That rookie season, Chad spent the nights before most games sleepless, staring at the ceiling in strange hotels in strange cities, Markbreit conked out on his queen-size bed a few feet away. A thousand questions danced through Chad's head, leading off with, *Why is this so hard?* followed by, *Why the hell am I here?* and nearly always ending with the quasi-metaphysical query: *What is holding?*

He knew this much. In the National Football League, the officials allowed offensive linemen to be extremely liberal with their hands. In the center of the line, huge taped hands the size of catchers' mitts flailed all over the place. There were more slaps, slashes, pokes, punches, and swipes than in a Jackie Chan movie. Holding, then, seemed defined by the only two things you *couldn't* do: wrestle the defender to the ground and rip his jersey off. In his second or third game, Chad watched an offensive guard shove, push, and grab the onrushing nose tackle. Chad dropped his flag. The guard rushed right over to him.

"Are you kidding me?" he screamed. "What a bad call! That was not holding! Hell, I don't think you even know what holding is!"

Chad adjusted the brim of his cap and walked away. *Asshole was right. I really don't know what holding is. Damn. I'm probably going to be on Seeman's training tape again.* He was right about that. *Jesus,* thought Chad, sitting with his crew, viewing the tape. *It's like I have my own weekly show. Sifferman's probably working on a name. I'll help him out. How about* "Bubba's Bloopers?"

Gradually, Chad began to distinguish between normal, everyday brutal line play and blatant holding. The night before the Raiders–Broncos game, Chad lay in bed in his hotel room in Denver counting the cracks in the ceiling, occasionally distracted by Letterman wisecracking from inside a faux antique armoire. Insight sometimes travels in the middle of the night. Something suddenly clicked inside him.

I'm doing too much, Chad said to himself. *I'm trying to be the best umpire in the league my rookie season, and that's not gonna happen. From now on, I'm not*

gonna drop a flag unless I am absolutely 100 percent
positive I see the foul. And before I even do that I'm
gonna watch Jerry, see what he calls as holding.

It was not only a good plan; it was a breakthrough.
For the first time that season, Chad felt exhaustion, the
good kind, not the kind that lies on your eyelids like
weights. That's simply fatigue, depression's partner.
He'd been feeling that all season. What he felt now was
the kind of exhaustion that drifts over you after a hard
day's work. You welcome it, bring it over you like a
blanket, because you know you've earned it. He closed
his eyes, sighed. Somewhere in the distance he heard
Madonna coo and Letterman chortle. He began to drift
off into a fragile dream state, the state before sleep, be-
lieving finally, and perhaps for the first time since he got
Jerry Seeman's phone call six months ago, that he truly
belonged in the National Football League.

It was a brutal battle, as most Oakland–Denver clashes
are. Low-scoring, lots of defense, several injuries. Inside
the meat grinder, it was like a heavyweight street fight.
A couple of head butts, some random biting, an eye
gouge or two, a river of blood, plenty of screaming and
whining, but no holding. At least none that Chad saw.
Then midway in the third quarter Markbreit dropped a
flag.

"Holding, Number 77!" he called, pointing to the
Raiders' big right tackle.

"What?" the player howled, mopping some blood
from a gash under his eye.

Jerry stared at the tackle, daring him to complain. He
started to protest some more, thought better of it, shook
his head, and walked away. He wasn't really in the mood
to take on Markbreit. Something about him. Markbreit's
head reached maybe to the lineman's shoulder pads, but

the referee seemed tough, in command. It was his *presence*, Chad decided.

"It comes with my attitude, my knowledge of the rules, and my fast mouth," Jerry had told him earlier, at breakfast. "You have it, too, Chad, with your *size*."

Chad nodded. Once he earned the players' respect, he knew he could use his size to great advantage.

"Of course, the other thing is, always keep moving. Make your call, decisively, loudly, and then get the hell out of there." Jerry was laughing, but Chad knew he did not mean this advice as a joke.

On the field, Markbreit blew his whistle and signaled for an official's time-out. The Raiders' tight end lay curled on the ground in a fetal position, moaning and pointing to his groin area. Art Shell, the Raiders' head coach and former All-Pro offensive tackle, raced onto the field to attend to his fallen player.

"He's all right, Art," Jerry assured him. "He just got kicked in the nuts."

"Agghhh," moaned the tight end.

"You're all right, get up," Shell said as he ran right by him and walked over to Jerry and Chad.

Shell pointed to his tackle, the one who'd just been flagged for holding. Art, generally quiet and rarely a complainer, was livid.

"What kind of a hold was that?" he fumed.

Jerry shrugged. "Same thing you used to do when you were a player. Excuse me." Jerry stepped in front of him and counted off fifteen fat yards.

Shell dismissed Markbreit with a wave. He turned back toward the sideline, nearly tripping over the tight end who was now up on all fours, trying to catch his breath.

"Come on, get up," Shell commanded.

The right tackle caught up to him and walked a few

yards with him toward the sideline. "I wasn't holding, Coach," he assured him.

"You know why I was an All-Pro and you're not?" Shell asked, never breaking stride.

"No."

"I never got caught."

Now that Chad could tell the difference between holding and the normal day-to-day street brawl in the middle of the line, he assumed, wrongly, that he could relax. He was by no means out of the woods yet. He had several more habits to break, a passel of league mechanics to learn, and even, to some degree, a new officiating philosophy to adjust to, all of it under fire and all of it under the magnifying glass of Jerry Seeman and the National Football League. Chad's career was being viewed, literally, on TV every week. He was beginning to feel like Jim Carrey in *The Truman Show*. At home, after a game, he'd often wondered how many people could handle such scrutiny in their jobs. "I mean, can you imagine having every minute of your job videotaped, then viewed, studied, and finally *graded* by all of your peers?" he said to Deborah one night. "Nobody else in the world has to go through this kind of scrutiny. The FBI, the military, politicians, nobody."

"Maybe they should."

Chad laughed. "Yeah, maybe they should." But then he added somberly, "Sometimes I feel like my whole life is on *Candid Camera*."

"Think of it this way," Deborah said. "When you become the best umpire in the league, the rookies will be watching *you*. You'll be the one featured on the tapes making all the good calls."

"Hard to imagine that right now."

"Chad."

She had that look now. She was about to cut to the

chase, slice right through the bullshit. Deborah had a gift. Like Chad's, it had to do with her sight. In her case, it was the gift of *in*sight. She had the ability to case out a situation and, with her combination of keen intelligence and X-ray vision, see right to the core. Frankly, Chad found this quality of Deborah's incredibly sexy.

"Chad, what have you always told me?"

She answered for him.

"You've told me more times than I can count that it was your *calling* to become an umpire in the National Football League. You said that everything you have done in football, playing, officiating, *everything* up until now, has prepared you for this. Am I right?"

She had him. She was scolding him a little, but just a little. Mainly, she was giving him a boost, validating who he was as a person and the career path he'd chosen. Everyone needs a shot of that once in a while. Chad looked at Deborah and felt how lucky he was to have her in his corner. He could almost hear the self-pity sneak out the back door.

"Well, Deb, I may have said something along those lines. . . ."

"You're going to make it in the NFL, Chad. I =mean"—and here she smiled—"*Bubba*."

10
A CHOP OFF THE OLD BLOCK

One of the mechanics Chad had to learn in the National Football League had to do with ball rotation. Simply put, this was how the football was thrown into the referee for the spot, which meant where he placed the ball. Correct placement of the ball was crucial because it established the new line of scrimmage and determined whether or not a first down had been made. In college, Chad, as umpire, would always receive the football from the official who was closest to the ball at the end of the play and, depending on the location of the referee, would often spot the ball himself. In the National Football League, on Jerry Markbreit's crew, Chad rarely spotted the ball. Jerry instructed him to get the ball from the deep official, usually the side judge or the field judge, then quickly lateral it to him, so he could spot it. You'd better hit Jerry in his breadbasket, too, or you'd hear about it. The last thing Jerry Markbreit wanted to do on national television was leap up in the air like an idiot for a ball a mile over his head or chase down a squibber that was zigzagging away because you bounced it a foot in front of him.

Chad quickly learned that spotting the football was one of Jerry's favorite duties. He wasn't quite sure why. Maybe it had to do with Jerry's role as crew chief and wanting to be able to control the flow of the game. Or maybe he was a camera hound and knew that every thirty seconds, while he spotted the football or signaled for a first down, it was guaranteed that he would be on TV. Whatever the reason, Chad soon adjusted to the NFL style of ball rotation. He was always careful to throw a perfect underhand spiral, belt-high, not too hard, right into Jerry's awaiting hands, and to keep his distance from Jerry when he was spotting the ball, making sure Jerry's close-up never became a two-shot.

Another mechanic Chad needed to master was called the Banana. The man given credit for popularizing this technique was former Cleveland Browns head coach Nick Skorich, who worked in the league office and was known as the umpires' guru.

In college, when the ball was snapped, especially on a running play, the rule was: turn toward the play and do not move. In the National Football League, as the play develops, the umpire is taught to "open up" his body and move toward the ball, move within the flow of traffic. When drawn on a chalkboard with Xs and Os, the technique resembles a banana. It makes perfect sense. By moving in the Banana, the umpire automatically gets a better angle, a whole view of the play. In college, by remaining stationary, you become trapped by the action. As the play moves away from you, even though you may have your eyes glued in the proper vicinity, there is really no way to see fouls without moving. In the Banana, the umpire is always in position.

Chad saw the value of the Banana immediately. However, it was a bear to adopt. It felt weird moving out of the middle. And it was scary as hell during draw plays.

"The play's coming right up the gut and you're stuck there because, just like the defense, you've been faked out."

Chad was explaining the dangers of the Banana to Markbreit and former NFL umpire Gordie Wells one night at dinner.

Chad, a born umpire, utters his first word: "Holding!"

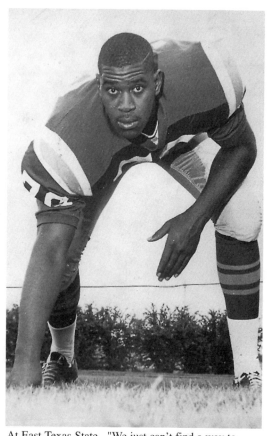

At East Texas State. "We just can't find a way to block him."

Coming out of East Texas State, Chad was All-American and an eventual draft pick of the Pittsburgh Steelers.

Playing for the New Orleans Saints, wondering: "Maybe I'd look better in stripes."

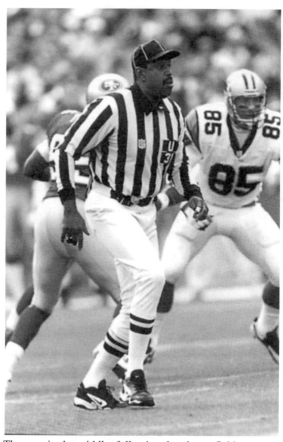

The man in the middle, following the play upfield.

(Photo credit: © 1998 Bill Nichols Photo Service)

In the meat grinder, arbitrating a "discussion" between an irate Buffalo Bill and a miffed Miami Dolphin.

(Photo credit: © NFL)

(*above*) Chad with Jerry Markbreit, either explaining a flag he has dropped or giving Jerry his lunch order.
(Photo credit: Richard Fitzer)

(*below*) In the grinder right before the snap, behind Junior Seau and facing John Elway. (Photo credit: Richard Fitzer)

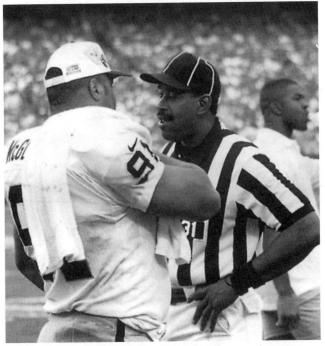

Chad and Chester McGlockton: "What do you mean that was a ten-cent call?" (Photo credit: Richard Fitzer)

Chad describing a call, in conference with George Hayward and referee Ed Hochuli.

(Photo credit: © 1998 Bill Nichols Photo Service)

"Well, it's a great way to get a whole view of the play," said Jerry.

"It's a great way to end up on your ass."

"Here's the thing, Chad," Gordie said. "As an umpire, you have to think of yourself as a linebacker."

Chad paused, his fork suspended in midair. He'd never considered this perspective before.

"You played the game," continued Gordie. "You just have to let your instincts take over. Keep your eyes on your guys, not the ball, and not the backfield. Your guys in the line will tell you the play by their feet. A guy fires forward, it's a run. He drops back, draw or pass. It's all instinct. It'll become second nature. The Banana helps you move with your guys. Then, in no time, using your instincts, you will *feel* if it's a draw play."

It's true, thought Chad. *You can feel whether it's about to be a draw play or a pass or a sweep.*

"You've got to learn the Banana," Jerry said. "The league has stressed that to me, over and over."

"Every umpire has to," added Gordie.

"It's a bitch to learn, man," said Chad. "Especially when you're used to *holding* your position. It's kind of like when you're learning to drive. You're told that if you go into a skid, you're supposed to turn in the direction of the skid. It doesn't sound right, doesn't feel right, but it's right. And it works."

"Same as the Banana." Gordie nodded.

"I'm gonna get it. Then I'm gonna perfect it."

"That's good," said Jerry, "and while you're doing that, perfect keeping your eyes off the quarterback. The league says every play you got your eyes in the back-field."

"Jesus Christ, Jerry, how can they possibly know where I got my eyes? How can they even see my eyes?"

"They're not looking at your eyes. They're looking

at the brim of your cap. And it's pointed straight into the damn backfield."

Gordie Wells grinned at Chad. "Big Brother's watching you, babe."

For most kids in elementary school, the best days of the week are Saturdays, Sundays, holidays, and snow days. The worst days, hands down, are the report card days. These days are filled with unspeakable suspense and immeasurable dread. One of the major advantages of adulthood, as we all discover, is that no matter what we do, we're not graded.

Unless, of course, you happen to be an NFL official.

The suspense returns and the dread reappears in the form of the weekly "game report," which indicates each penalty flag the official has thrown that week and grades each infraction from 1 (F) to 7 (A+). The league office sends each referee the game reports for his crew. He, in turn, mails or faxes them to each official. Wednesday, and sometimes Thursday, each week, all season long, is report card day.

His rookie year, on the Wednesday following the Atlanta Falcons–New Orleans Saints game, Chad sat in his office in the John Wooden Center at UCLA in an unfamiliar state of calm. For the first time all season, he was actually looking forward to his game report. He felt no pressure and no fear. It was as if he'd studied weeks for an exam, taken it, and blasted through the test like Terrell Davis galloping through the Chicago Bears. Chad knew he'd aced it. The previous Sunday in New Orleans he'd had his first good game in the National Football League. Check that. It was his first *great* game. Damn, he felt good. *Bring on the game report, baby, bring it onnn!*

The phone rang in his office. *What now? Probably my boss. Why does he always bother me at work?*

Chad answered the phone.

"Chad."

"Chad *Brown*?"

Not his boss. The voice was familiar, though. Someone of authority, that's for sure.

"This is Jack Reader, supervisor of officials."

Chad beamed into the phone. He knew what was coming. Reader was the supervisor in the league office who personally graded the tapes. Obviously, Reader was calling to congratulate him on last week's game. *I'm on my way now*, thought Chad. *I wonder how many rookies get invited to do the Super Bowl? I'm probably shooting too high. Give me a league championship game my first year; then next year I'll go to the Super Bowl. Yeah, don't want to get cocky. God, that game felt so good. So right. Everything was clicking. The mechanics, the moves, the spots, the discussions with Jerry. Talked him into one foul, out of another. Hell, I even got the Banana down cold.*

."Yeah, this is Chad Brown. How ya doin', Jack?"

"Get out a paper and pencil right now. You missed four calls in that ball game last week. *Four* of 'em."

Reader must have dialed the wrong number. Chad waited for Reader to realize his mistake.

"You there, Chad?"

Nope. Right number.

"Yeah. I'm here. . . ." Chad's spirits sank like an anchor.

"You missed a face mask, a takedown, and two holding calls. Get out a *pencil*."

Chad scoured the top of his desk. It was bare except for his NFL schedule and a picture of Deborah and the boys. No pencil. He whipped open his letter drawer and rummaged through it. No pencil. He flung open each side drawer and riffled through them. No pencil. He pulled out the file drawer and burrowed through that like

a transient going through a garbage can. A bag of Chee-
tos. An electric shaver. A couple of hand weights. A
stapler. A Scotch tape dispenser. An old copy of *Referee
Magazine*. Nothing *resembling* a pencil.

"You got a pencil?"

"Yes, sir, right here," Chad said.

"Write these down."

Reader began to list the first of Chad's missed fouls
in exquisite detail.

Then Chad saw it. Not a pencil. A red ink marker. A
permanent red ink marker. *Thank God, I can write these
down.* He exhaled a small wind of relief. But then he
realized he had no paper.

HOW CAN I HAVE AN OFFICE WITH NO PAPER
AND NO PENCIL?

*Calm down, calm down. They've got to be in here
somewhere. But where the hell are they? Come on, think.
You know this place like the back of your hand.*

The back of my . . . Sigh. *It'll have to do. . . .*

Suddenly writing with the speed of a court reporter,
Chad began scribbling the excruciatingly detailed list of
the fouls he missed on the back of his hand.

That night, at home, Deborah Brown sent her sons,
Devin and Trent, into the bathroom to wash their hands
for dinner.

"We can't," said Devin. "Daddy's still in there washing *his* hands."

"What's all that red stuff on 'em?" asked Trent.

"Homework," explained Deborah.

In the bathroom, as Chad tried, in vain, to scrub off
the list of fouls Jack Reader had given him, he paused
and stared at his reflection in the mirror.

Mirror, mirror, on the wall . . .

Is it time for me to look for another line of work?

*   *   *

The point at which it all changed for Chad, the instant that the momentum shifted, came, as in a football game, when he least expected it.

It happened one freezing cold afternoon in New York. It was the last game of Chad's rookie season. The New York Giants were playing the Dallas Cowboys. The bitterness of the day was matched by the bitterness of the rivalry. This was a crucial game; the winner would be the Eastern Conference champion and would receive home field advantage throughout the play-offs.

Chad spent this day in the meat grinder, today more like a meat *locker*, dressed for arctic conditions. He wore gloves, long johns, thermal socks, earmuffs, and a long-sleeve turtleneck beneath his stripes. It made little difference. His cheeks felt as if they were being stung with a thousand icy little needles. The metal of his whistle was so cold it nearly burned his shivering lips.

It was late in the game. Dallas had a one-point lead, but the Giants were on the move. They put together two quick first downs. One more first down and they would be in field goal range. The game would be theirs.

The Giants' quarterback dropped back to pass. He pumped his arm once, twice, desperately looking for an open receiver. The exhausted and bloodied offensive line fought off the ferocious Dallas pass rush.

And then Chad saw it. Blatant, unmistakable. Right in front of him.

A chop block.

Disguised cleverly. Because it was the center and the *tackle*, not the guard, who was involved in the tag team. The tackle was the setup man. He blocked the pass rusher high, distracting him. The center sneaked in behind him and hit him low. His legs cut out from under him, the Dallas defender toppled over backward and disappeared, buried beneath a pile of bodies.

Chad reached into his belt and threw his flag, at the

same instant a Giant receiver gathered in a pass at the sideline. First down.

But wait.

Flag on the play, in the middle of the line. The crowd, on their feet, insane, stomping, screaming to ward off the cold and the Cowboys, began to register mass outrage against what they knew was a drive-killing call. They eyed the umpire with murder in their collective 120,000 eyes.

Jerry hustled over to Chad. "What do you got?"

"I got a chop block, Jerry."

Markbreit arched his head up toward Chad. For the first time that season, for the first time since he'd known him, Jerry's eyes turned hard. "It better be there."

"Yeah, it is, Jerry. I *know* I saw it."

At that moment, in the middle of the Meadowlands, Chad Brown experienced a brief history of time. An entire season of training tapes, blown calls, new techniques, and confidence boosts from wife, family, and crew shot through his head like a psychedelic triptych. He tilted his head toward Jerry. He could almost feel Jerry's eyes boring into his skull. Then he saw Jerry nod. He was going with him. Even more important, he believed him.

Markbreit, cradling the football like a baby, dashed over to the line of scrimmage. He signaled the penalty.

"Illegal chop block. . . ."

Dan Reeves, the head coach of the Giants, ripped off his headset and spiked it into the ground. He was beyond nuts. He was having a tantrum, and he was inconsolable.

"A *chop block?!* Are you crazy?! My players never *ever* chop block! It's our season, goddammit! Jesus Christ! A chop block! I don't believe it, Markbreit!"

As Jerry moved the Giants fifteen yards back, out of field goal range, Reeves stalked him on the sideline, matching him step for step.

"This is totally wrong. I can't let you do this, Jerry. My players never chop. You hear me? Look at me, goddammit! Are you listening to me? Jerry? *JERRY!*"

Then, as Jerry had instructed Chad, he ignored Reeves, waded back into the action of the field, rotated his arms to get the clock going again.

What if it's not there? Chad thought. He absently rubbed his cheeks, trying to stop the stabbing of those vicious little ice needles.

"Well," Chad said aloud. "I guess that was either the beginning of my career in the NFL or the end."

"They're killing us in New York, kid."

Chad's chair squeaked as he leaned back and rubbed his forehead. It was Monday, the Day After. Jerry was on the phone.

"The papers, talk shows, even the goddamn *Today Show.* We're assholes, we're screwups, we're the reason the Giants lost the division."

"Jesus."

"Oh, yeah. They're way up our ass."

"What about Reeves?"

"Nuts. Out of his mind. My players don't chop, there was no chopping in that game. . . . He called it the worst officiating ever. Said it's tough enough playing the Dallas Cowboys without also having to worry about the officials. Here's one of his milder quotes: 'I don't know what umpire Chad Brown saw, but it sure wasn't a chop block. I feel like we got the shaft.' "

The line went silent for about ten seconds. Chad knew what Jerry was about to ask.

"It's there, right, Chad? The chop block is there? We're going to see it when we look at the tape. Right?"

"I'm telling you, Jerry . . . no, I *promise* you. . . . How's this? I *guarantee* you. It's there."

*   *   *

It wasn't there.

Seeman, Markbreit, and two NFL supervisors, former officials, all watched the tape three times without seeing a chop block, then they ordered lunch, and, over deli sandwiches and coffee, watched it again. They went to slow motion, paused the action, and even zoomed in. Still no sign of a chop. All they saw was plenty of bruising line play, weirdly juxtaposed against a tableau of snow flurries.

Markbreit ran his hand through his substantial hair. Jesus. Sleigh bells ringing. Children singing. Welcome to a winter wonderland.

"Well," Seeman proclaimed gravely. "I don't see it." He looked at Markbreit.

"Chad saw it. It's there. I know it's there."

"Did you see it?"

"No," Markbreit admitted. But he believed Chad and he believed in his crew. Every official in the league was once a rookie and went through a season of adjustment. This wasn't about that. Chad was too passionate about seeing the chop. Too definite. He was going to bet that Chad, the ex–NFL lineman, knew a chop block when he saw one. And that even in the midst of the freezing cold and swirling snow, Chad wasn't prone to seeing a mirage. It *was* there.

"What do you want me to do, run the tape again?" Seeman asked, but it was more of a challenge.

"No," Markbreit said. "Let's take a break."

The supervisors stood, stretched, started out. Markbreit hesitated, turned back to Seeman.

"What if we don't see it? You gonna cut him some slack?"

"Been cutting him slack all year."

"It's there, Jerry," Markbreit insisted. "It just may not be on camera."

Seeman shrugged. It was a gesture that did not suggest ignorance. It suggested, instead, *If the chop block's not there, we're gonna have to deal with Chad Brown.*

Markbreit and the others watched the tape one more time and saw no evidence of a chop block. Frustrated, Seeman sent everyone home, saying he would make a decision later in the week about Chad.

"What does it mean, Jerry?" Chad asked him during one of their several phone calls that week.

"It doesn't mean a thing, kid," Markbreit lied. "Seeman'll grade you down. Maybe he'll call you, give you a hard time. Don't lose sleep over it."

Too late. Chad had already lost plenty of sleep over it. Hell, he hadn't slept all season.

"Just tell me," Chad said. "Are they gonna bust me out of the league?"

"No. You're a good umpire."

Chad wasn't sure he believed him but let it pass. "I saw it. I'm telling you, Jerry, I saw it."

"I believe you, kid. We'll handle this." He didn't sound very convincing to either Chad or, for that matter, to himself.

The next night, Jerry Markbreit got an excited phone call from Terry Gierke, the head linesman on his crew. Terry taped every game he worked for his personal collection. He knew of the controversy surrounding the chop block and decided to watch his own tape. Maybe he could see something Seeman and the supervisors didn't.

"Hey, Jer, I gotta tell you, it's right there. In plain sight. I don't know how you guys missed it."

"You see the chop?"

"Oh, yeah. The tackle and center. Guy goes down like a ton of bricks. Lucky he didn't snap a knee."

"Overnight the tape to me, will you, Terry?"

"You got it."

"You're saving the kid's ass. And mine."

"Gotta look out for our crew."

Terry Gierke sent the tape to Markbreit, who viewed it, shouted out loud when he saw the chop block, cued it up, FedExed it to Seeman, who watched it, shook his head, called Dan Reeves and told him it was there, Chad was right, called Markbreit, who called Chad.

"Some reason the network feed was different. Or we were looking in the wrong place. Who the hell knows? Point is, it was there. Mr. Chop Block."

"Wow," said Chad. "I gotta tell you, Jerry, I was sweating bullets, weren't you?"

"Nah. I always knew it was there."

Chad laughed. "Yeah, right. What did Seeman say?"

Markbreit paused for effect. Then he said what were, to every official in the National Football League, the two sweetest words in the English language.

"Good call."

THIRD QUARTER
V

11
A DAY IN THE LIFE

Chad peers at the locker-room clock. Two minutes to go in halftime. Two minutes before the Carolina Panthers resume their war with the San Francisco 49ers. Time for the most dreaded part of the umpire's job.

The substance check.

Before each game and at halftime, the umpire is required to check four players at random from each team for illegal foreign substances on their uniforms. A few years ago, some players were caught with silicone sprayed on their jerseys, making their uniforms slippery and difficult to grab. In previous seasons, Chad had heard rumors of players applying a veritable pantry of cooking substances onto their uniforms, including butter, margarine, Mazola oil, olive oil, safflower oil, and, apparently the league favorite, PAM cooking oil spray. He'd even heard of one lineman who swathed his jersey with Vaseline and kept a wad of the goo shmooshed under each armpit so that he was sure to keep his jersey properly lubricated during the game. Despite the rumors, in seven years of foreign substance checks, Chad had yet to find a single trace of anything. *Still, it's part of my job,* he thought, *just as making sure before each game that the air pressure of all twenty footballs is no more than 13 pounds.*

Chad stands outside the San Francisco locker room and waits for the four players to arrive. They do—Bryant

Young, Derrick Deese, Roy Barker, and, of course, Kevin Gogan.

Chad looks up to the sky. Why Gogan? This is so stupid. He sighs and begins patting down each player.

"This is Chad's favorite part," Gogan says. "The frisk."

"You were hoping for this, right, Goge?" says Chad.

Gogan—all 350 pounds—steps forward. Chad begins patting down his jersey.

"You shoulda seen me before I had silicone," says Gogan. "I had no tits."

"And now you look just like Pamela Sue Anderson," says Chad.

"Jealous?"

"You're clean."

"Thank you, honey." And Kevin Gogan, *Sports Illustrated*'s dirtiest player in the National Football League, sashays onto the field.

"Substance check?" a voice behind Chad asks.

Chad turns. It's Steve Mariucci, head coach of the 49ers.

"Yeah, coach."

"You're wasting your time."

"Part of my job description," says Chad.

Third quarter. Shadows blanket the field. Most of the fans are on their feet as Carolina kicks to the 49ers' R. W. McQuarters. Chad settles in. Twenty more minutes of football.

Well, not really.

Chad has done the math, and he knows, in fact, that there are only thirteen minutes of actual football played in every game. The other forty-seven minutes are made up of climbing off of and out of piles of players, standing in huddles, and walking back and forth to the line of scrimmage. The total concentrated amount of time remaining in this game is exactly six and a half minutes.

McQuarters catches the ball at his own fifteen-yard line and blazes toward his right, running across the whole field, past his wall of blockers. He flashes upfield. He's at the twenty, the twenty-five, the thirty—and into the clear. Chad runs to the play. R.W. has one man to beat, John Kasay, the kicker. He veers back toward the middle and is blindsided by the last Carolina man.

"Jesus. What a hit," Chad says to George Hayward, the head linesman.

"I didn't see anything, did you?" Hayward asks.

"No," Chad says gently.

Hayward is eager, enthusiastic. He nods, jogs back to his position.

"Ball!" Chad shouts.

McQuarters tosses the ball to Chad as he's engulfed by a flood of teammates. The offense returns, ready to take over on the forty. Chad spots the ball, just shy of the hash mark.

"*That's* the spot?" Mariucci shouts from the sideline. "You're shorting me, Chad!"

"Don't short the boss." It's Gogan. He smiles at Chad.

Chad sighs. "Damn, Gogan. You make it hard to do my *job*. . . ."

Chad Brown leans his forearms onto his metal desk. His eyes lock into yours.

"This is not my *job*," he says with conviction. "It's more. It's my career. I take it very seriously. I work hard at it. Put in a lot of hours."

He hesitates. Chad is a modest man. He doesn't want what he's about to say to be taken as anything close to arrogance. But there is pride. Enormous pride. He is proud he survived his rookie season, proud he has improved each year, and proud of his current status in the National Football League.

"I went through hell to get where I am. Especially that first year. But I think, after seven years in the league," he says quietly, "I'm one of the best umpires in the game."

There, done. He's said it. But there's one more thing.

"It really doesn't matter what you think. You're not the best until someone you respect tells you you're the best. Then you know you've made it."

He leans back now, finished with that. He glances at the ceiling for a second, then lowers his eyes back into yours.

"You know what bothers me the most? That the fans don't know what we go through before each game. They're unaware of the preparation. I think some of them believe we're just dropped off at the stadium each week, handed a striped shirt, and told, 'Good luck, go officiate the game.' There is a helluva lot more to it than that. A helluva lot more. . . ."

November 23, 1998. *Monday Night Football.* Miami Dolphins at the New England Patriots.

A typical week.

It begins, as every week does, with bodywork. A minimum of two hours a day, five days a week. In the off-season, Chad adds a day, resting only on Sunday. He starts with a mile-and-a-half run as a warm-up. Every other day, he does another two or three miles of sprints, usually two twenties on a track, either right after the warm-up run or separately, in the afternoon. Then the real fun begins.

Most days, as he has for the last two years, he'll meet his workout buddy, Doug Erickson, an administrative assistant at UCLA and dedicated weight lifter, for serious weight training. Before Doug, Chad's routine centered on rather random and aimless heavy lifting. Doug saw that Chad needed direction. He adjusted his workout to one that concentrates on a different part of the body every session.

It breaks down like this: Monday: chest, including bench presses, several sets of six to eight repetitions using 220 pounds; Tuesday: upper body, shoulders, arms, chest; Wednesday: legs, workout finishing with killer full squats and murderous sets of calf lifts; Thursday: arms, nothing fancy, mainly curls; Friday: shoulders, military press, pull-downs, rowing—torture. Every day is ab day. Sit-ups, crunches, more rowing. Not Chad's favorite. Not anyone's favorite. Doug also redesigned Chad's diet. He now avoids fatty foods, fried foods, most sweets. The diet is heavy on protein and salads, light on starch.

So much for the myth of the overweight, out-of-shape NFL official. Chad is in better shape than 90 percent of the population, certainly for his age, and works out as much as most players.

Next, the mental prep. It starts with the weekly take-home exam. Every week of the season, every official is required to take an open-book exam. The book used is the official NFL rule book. The exam normally consists of fifty questions, twenty true-or-false, the rest short-answer or multiple-choice. The subjects covered include passing, rushing, kicking, and penalty enforcement. As in most open-book tests, it's harder than you would think. Chad takes the test carefully. He knows that the answers will be discussed each week during the pregame crew meetings. Chad sets time aside Tuesday or Wednesday night to work on his test. All told, completing the test could take two hours or more.

Chad's flight out of Los Angeles for the Monday night game in New England is scheduled to leave at 11:15 Sunday morning. Saturday night, Chad packs two carry-on bags. The first is a briefcase containing his weekly exam, some reading material, plane tickets, parking passes, and the weekly paper storm sent to him by the league office. In the eye of the storm is the weekly referees' report compiled by Jerry Seeman, which includes comments on physical signals about fouls ("Please work diligently in this area."), dead ball officiating ("Never quit. Downfield officials must 'accordion' on all plays ending near the line of scrimmage."), tips for the umpire ("When an umpire marks off a penalty, never do it diagonally when coming in from a side zone. Always square off."), and a warning for off-officials assisting on calls ("Basic mechanics dictate that an off-official is involved in a call *only* if 100 percent sure. Never come in and muddy the waters."). The storm also designates which players will be tested for foreign substances, details a list of administrative matters, and closes with a locker-room type of pep talk: "You do an admirable job and are to be complimented for the professional way you handle yourself. This week, for example, there was *ONE* play that drew national attention out of the nearly 2,400 plays." Also swirling in the storm of papers are the weekend schedule, a timing report, the 1994–98 cumulative accepted penalty summary report, the 1998 kickoff analysis/try attempts, the weekly game travel/itinerary sheet, and the list of 1998 players wearing eye shields (tinted or clear).

The other bag Chad packs is a small suitcase, which contains his street clothes and his uniform and the rest of his personal equipment for the game. Chad, a meticulous man, approaches this task with military care and precision. He washes his uniform personally. No way he will trust a dry cleaner. Garments have been known to come back soiled, torn, late, or not at all. After washing, drying, and ironing his zebra shirt and pants, Chad folds them with creases as sharp as razor blades. He polishes his shoes, as he does weekly, using Armor All to guard them from the elements and get them gleaming like glass, so clear you can see your reflection in them.

He goes on the Internet and checks the weather in Boston. The game will be played on the Monday before Thanksgiving. No snow is forecast. It's predicted to be unseasonably warm, about forty degrees at game time, clear skies, no wind. Still, it's long john weather. He folds in an extra pair of heavy wool socks, his long-sleeve shirt, jock, and the rest of the tools of his trade: hat, whistle, penalty flag, and his blue beanbag to mark fumbles.

Next Chad packs his pregame attire. The National Football League has an unofficial dress code for officials, which mirrors its unwritten, but often-quoted, off-field code of conduct: "You are always an official. You must act the part. Be cautious of your conversation in public places, maintain an air of professionalism at all times, and on the day of the game, especially on the way to the game, business attire is required."

On Markbreit's crew, business attire meant a sport jacket and tie. Ed Hochuli is a turtleneck man. His crew, Chad among them, has adopted the Hochuli look—a solid dark-colored lightweight wool mock turtleneck beneath a sport jacket. At first, Chad thought the crew resembled a sixties singing groups like the Platters or the Association. By the end of preseason, Chad and the rest of the crew not only felt more comfortable in their turtlenecks than in the traditional shirt and tie, they also decided they looked sharp. Which they do. One of the more passionate discussions of the week now inevitably revolves around where to buy the best turtlenecks (including mail-order and online), a quality turtleneck being defined as one that had a good weave, an affordable price, and a minimum of neck itch.

Sunday morning, November 22, Chad says his good-byes to Deborah and the boys. This is the hardest part for Chad. Weekends are family time. Chad is a devoted homebody and a true hands-on dad. He feels that every time he steps out the door to catch a plane, he's missing a part of his sons' childhood.

Chad drives himself to the airport. No limo, no cab, no car service. He'll spend the rest of the weekend being a passenger in someone else's car. He'll be driven from the airport to the hotel, from the hotel to the stadium, then back to the airport. Chad prefers to be at the wheel. This is the only chance he'll have in the next two days to drive. He takes advantage of it; he drives slower than usual and cranks up his custom sound system to max.

The NFL asks that the officials arrive in the home team's city at least twenty-four hours before kickoff. Occasionally members of Chad's crew will spend a day or two in a city before the first crew meeting. Usually it's because they want to visit family, as Chad did when there was a game in Dallas, or take in a Broadway play in New York or soak up the sights in interesting cities like Washington, D.C. or San Francisco. Chad rarely indulges in these side trips. He is all business. Fly in, check in, meet the crew, go through all the pregame stuff, suit up, do the game, take a shower, and get the hell out of Dodge.

Chad is an indifferent flyer. He's never afraid, never thrilled, mostly bored. The main benefit is that the officials fly first-class. There is a difference: better food, more legroom, and dibs on the good cookies, snacks, and drinks. He always sits by the window. The only disadvantage to this is playing Russian roulette in terms of who might sit next to him. First-class tickets are expensive, but as of yet there is no personality requirement to get in. The most welcome sight to Chad at takeoff is an empty seat next to him. This day, though, as the jet noses upward into the clouds, beginning the six-hour flight to Boston, Chad hears:

"You with the NFL?"

Chad glances at the passenger next to him. He's a stubby man flaunting more jewelry than a display case at Tiffany's. He reeks of Canoe.

"What?"

"You must be with the NFL." With his pinkie finger, the passenger points at the NFL rule book Chad is studying.

"Oh, yeah. I am."

Chad deliberately buries his head in the rule book. *I'm gonna be cold to this guy. Ice-cold. I know the type. I ignore him, show him I'm not interested in having a conversation, he'll leave me alone. Give Rocket the hard shoulder. I'll give this guy the cold shoulder.*

"So whataya do in the NFL? You a player? Nah. You're too old. Wait a minute. I know you."

Chad gives up. He closes the rule book and smiles at the guy.

"You're Gene Upshaw, right?"

"No."

"Yes, you are. Don't bullshit me. Howya doin,' Gene? Mike Fitch. Chicopee, Mass. Out here on business."

"I'm not Gene Upshaw. I'm Chad Brown. I'm an NFL official."

"Whoa. Really? An NFL official?"

"Yes."

"No shit. Can I be blunt? You guys have been royally fucking up all year. That call in New York? Gimme a break. The quarterback missed the goal line by a fuckin' *foot*. What was his name?"

"Vinny Testaverde."

"No, that's not it. And the coin toss in Detroit? Did you see that?"

"Yeah, I did."

"What the hell happened there? Jesus Christ, how do

you blow a coin flip? You didn't have anything to do with that, did you?"

"No, I—"

"Can I buy you a drink?"

"No. Thanks. Listen, Mike, I've got to get back to my test—"

"You get tested?"

"Every week. Part of my job."

"Really? That is fascinating. I'll tell you this, you do not have an easy job, am I right?"

"You're right about that."

"Can I ask you a personal question? I assume you're married, good-looking guy like you—"

"Yes, I'm married. Got two kids."

"Excellent. Perfect. Now here's my question. Are you prepared for when you pass on? Because that's what I do, estate planning. You think you're gonna live forever? You're not. You're gonna die just like everybody else. Could happen right on the field, could be tomorrow. One of those huge, pardon my French, mofo linemen comes at you, you're not looking, *wham bam!* Next thing you know, they're carrying you off the field on a stretcher, and instead of wearing a turtleneck, you're wearing a neck collar. You gotta plan, Thad."

"Chad."

Help! I'm trapped! Chad hollers to himself.

"I got a brochure. . . ."

Jesus. Next time I'm going to buy the whole row.

12
DRUG TEST

Six hours later, after feigning a four-hour nap, a colorful estate planning and annuity proposal tucked under his arm, Chad shakes hands with Mike Fitch from Chicopee, Mass., and ducks into an awaiting airport van bound for the Logan Airport Ramada. He feels as if he's just coming up for air after having been trapped in a locked safe under the sea. In the van, he peers at the weekend schedule. He's the second from his crew to arrive. George Hayward, the head linesman, came in at 1:30 this afternoon. A quick glance at the schedule outlines their meetings, mealtimes, and departure time for Foxboro Stadium. Hold on a sec. They're leaving at 4:45 for an 8:20 start? Then Chad remembers they're in Boston, the worst city in the league in terms of stadium proximity to the airport. It could take an hour, easy, to get there, maybe even more in rush-hour traffic. He thinks of the other problem places to play.

The first place that comes to mind is New York. Forget New York City. The Giants and Jets don't even play in New York *State*. They play in New Jersey, in the Meadowlands, which is about an hour from the airport, usually in horrible traffic, and you can't drive with your windows open because there's a strange stench that gets worse the closer you get to the stadium. *I'll take smog over that smell any day.* Then there are the Detroit Lions, who don't play anywhere near Detroit. They play in

Pontiac, which is another hour from the Detroit Airport, in the middle of nowhere. At least they're building a brand-new stadium complex in downtown Detroit, which will cut travel time in half and is supposed to be state-of-the-art.

He stares out the window and thinks about each city and stadium. Just for fun, he decides to rate them from best to worst. The best stadium locker rooms for officials are without a doubt in New Orleans and Indianapolis. Each official has an individual room, with a private shower. Dallas has the best food, offering a huge pre- and postgame buffet. The hotel they stay in when they travel to Miami is by far the best, wonderfully appointed, with a spectacular view of the ocean and harbor, lined with million-dollar yachts. The best city for restaurants and nightlife, a close third behind New York and New Orleans is, surprisingly, Atlanta.

• Now the worst. Hands down, the grubbiest locker room in the league is where they'll be working tomorrow, New England's Foxboro Stadium. The second worst in the league is the rat hole masquerading as a locker room in Jacksonville. The rest of the officials' locker rooms, with the exceptions of the ones in Indianapolis, New Orleans, and Dallas, are all in a dead heat for just plain bad.

Chad checks into his hotel room at the Ramada, kicks off his shoes, lies on his bed, picks up the remote, and clicks on the television. He channel surfs through the local stations, glances at the news, finally settles on a wrap-up of the day's football action and college basketball games on *SportsCenter*. He yawns. It's amazing. He always gets more tired sitting in an airplane doing nothing for six hours than working his butt off in the weight room for two hours. Maybe it's the time difference. Or maybe it's being cooped up here at the Logan Airport Ramada, alone, suddenly missing his family desperately, with nothing to do until the dinner meeting with the crew, which isn't happening for another hour and a half. He yawns again. Damn. If it weren't so cold outside, he'd go for a run. *Yeah, right. Where? Up and down the runway? I'll zone out with the tube. Jesus. Nothing on but a bunch of crap. An old black-and-white musical, some kid's movie, a million reruns, golf—now there's a spectator sport—wrestling, and a Korean game show. Man. I'd call home, but I think Deborah took the kids somewhere, bowling or to a birthday party.* He yawns again. This part, the waiting, is the worst part. He phones the front desk and arranges for a wake-up call in an hour. He closes his eyes and tries to sleep for real this time, but all he manages to do is stare at the ceiling like when he was a rookie in a hundred hotel rooms just like this one, feeling anxious, wound up, wanting to *go*.

The whole crew, minus Ed Hochuli, the referee, and Tom Fincken, the side judge, whose flight doesn't arrive until nearly ten o'clock, sit together in the Ramada's main dining room. Chad sits between Don Carey, the back judge, and Bill Spyksma, the line judge. The conversation begins, as it normally does among these five men, with small talk and gossip. No one talks football yet. There is the mandatory, "How was your flight?" Chad simply shakes his head. He doesn't want to relive *that*. As the salads come, Spyksma goes over the itinerary. Carey and Pete Morelli, the field judge, remind the others that they're in charge of transportation from the hotel to the stadium, which means they arrange for the cars and drive them to Foxboro. If given the choice, Chad would drive himself. Carey drives like a maniac, and Morelli drives like an eighty-year-old woman with cataracts.

By the main course and into dessert the discussion shifts to the weekly test. As always, the dinner will become an informal review session. George Hayward, the head linesman, is in charge of testing. He will bring up the trickier test questions on that week's exam. Someone will offer his answer and how he got it. There will be disagreement and debate. If a fine point of a rule is in question, each official will argue and defend his interpretation. A consensus, sometimes a reluctant one, will be reached. Chad finds the review helpful. It prepares him for the morning meeting tomorrow, game day, when they will go over the test for real with Hochuli.

A waiter clears their plates.

"Hey, Chad," Morelli says. "I got a problem. I need four tickets for next week's game in Chicago."

"Wait a minute. I gave you four tickets."

"I know. I need four more."

"Well, does anybody want to give his up?"

"I'll give up one," says Hayward.

"I actually need two more myself," says Carey. "I just didn't want to be greedy." He looks at Morelli.

The rest of the guys laugh.

"If you switch mine for the Chicago game, I'll switch off with you for the New Orleans game in two weeks," offers Spyksma.

"Forget it. I want extras for New Orleans."

"Damn," says Chad. "I need two more for the Dallas game on the twentieth."

"I'll give you my two for Dallas, you give me your two for New Orleans," says Spyksma.

"Done," says Chad.

"Hey," says Morelli, "what about my four for Chicago?"

Chad rubs his forehead. He's getting a headache. For the past four seasons, the last three with Markbreit's crew and this year with Hochuli's, Chad has been in charge of tickets. It's a thankless job. At first, he thought it would be a perfect fit for him because of his gift for organization. Unfortunately, officials receive a limited number of tickets for each game. There are often not enough tickets to go around. Certain games become prizes: the ones to great games and the ones to great cities. Being organized is only half the battle. The man handling the tickets also has to be a tough negotiator.

"Can we deal with this later?" suggests Chad. "I'd like to go over the test."

Murmurs of agreement. As the others fumble through coats and snap open briefcases in search of their exam sheets, Chad considers how the crew functions: *We're all part of a system, Hochuli's system now, Markbreit's before. They both work. The truth is, when we're clicking, we're a well-oiled machine, both on and off the field. As long as you take care of business, do your job, watch your back, cover your ass, and, on occasion, cover the ass of anyone on the crew who's exposed, we more than click; we rock.* He thinks about each man's dual role:

Ed Hochuli: referee, film sessions.
Chad Brown: umpire, tickets (pain in the rear).
George Hayward: head linesman, weekly testing.
Pete Morelli: field judge, cars, VCR setup.
Bill Spyksma: line judge, weekly schedules.
Don Carey: back judge, transportation.
Tom Fincken: side judge, banker.

Three hours and about a pot of coffee later, Chad calls it a night. It's close to midnight East Coast time, but his body is still on West Coast time, where it's not even nine o'clock. Chad has found that on the quick trip out of town it's better to stay up late to avoid getting jet lag. This has been an intense day. The six-hour plane flight, the exam review, seemingly more heated than usual, and straightening out everyone's ticket requests, all combined with missing a workout, have left Chad feeling wasted. Rubbing his eyes, he enters his hotel room, eager to crash, looking forward to a good night's sleep.

The flashing red message light on the phone stops him.

He watches it for a few seconds, its urgent red beacon blinking on and off, on and off, and tries to imagine who could have left him a message. He prays it's not Deborah. For seven years, his one dread has been there will be an emergency with someone in his family and he's trapped in New York or New England, three thousand miles away. He picks up the phone, dials in for the message. Voice trembling, he gives his room number. It's got to be Deborah. Who else could it be?

"Chad? It's Ed Hochuli. Guess what we've got tomorrow morning between six and seven A.M.? That's right. Drug test. Room Three Forty-two. Have a nice night!"

He is instantly filled with relief that the call didn't come from California. He yawns, really tired now, longing to drift off to sleep. Drug test. Now that's something to look forward to.

But par for the course. The National Football League enforces random drug testing on all players and officials. Officials are never told when a drug test will occur. You're simply told to report to a certain room at a certain time and pee in a cup in front of a total stranger. *Not my idea of a good time,* smirks Chad, *but another necessary rule of the NFL. Man, am I tired.* A chorus of men's voices screaming of rule intricacies and variations reverberates in his head. Chad distances himself just enough from the sound to call the front desk and arrange for a 6:30 wake-up call. Then he collapses onto his bed. Despite the steady stream of coffee, he's fast asleep in a matter of minutes.

Chad wakes at five-thirty in the morning to go to the bathroom. In a half-dream state, he slides into the bathroom and, without giving it a moment's thought, relieves himself. Finished, his bladder empty, he heads back to bed. He yawns again.

Maybe I can go back to sleep, catch another hour before I have to take my . . .

Drug test.

Oh, this is great. Perfect.

I just gave away all my urine.

Panicked, he finds some clothes and slaps them on.

The hotel dining room is, surprise of surprises, deserted at five-thirty in the morning. Chad, a newspaper tucked under his arm, approaches the only person in sight, a forty-fivish waitress with skin the color of Liquid Paper, droopy eyes under eyelids resembling tiny blue awnings, and a face with a lot of miles on it. She's somehow managed to fold herself into a rumpled white uniform and silly paper hat.

"Anywhere," she says.

"I know what I want," says Chad, plunking himself down at a table.

The waitress shrugs, flips over her order pad.

"Give me a large orange juice, large grapefruit juice, a pitcher of water, and a pot of coffee."

"What are you, on some kind of fast?"

"Look, I'm kind of in a hurry."

"Not a problem. I don't think the kitchen's too busy right now."

The waitress disappears, then returns in a flash, balancing Chad's drinks on a tray.

"Thanks."

He chugs the water, drains the orange juice, and starts working on the coffee. The waitress lounges at the next table, her legs crossed, one leg seesawing like a bony windmill. She eyes Chad with fascination.

Chad swigs down half the grapefruit juice and stares at her. "What?"

"Are you Gene Upshaw?"

"No," Chad sighs. "I'm not."

"I know you're somebody. Who are you?"

"You're right," Chad says. "I *am* somebody. I'm Dave Winfield."

After downing an amount of liquid roughly equivalent to what can be held in the bladder of a camel, Chad sloshes up to Room 342 for his drug test. Two slightly bored representatives from the National Football League's drug unit administer the test. The first guy, incongruously attired in a suit and latex gloves, has the dual role of both greeting each official as he comes into the room and collecting his cup of urine before he leaves. *Now that's gotta be the worst job in the world,* Chad thinks as he enters the room. *I guess someone has to do it.* The drug unit guy smiles too widely at Chad.

Chad's got a problem. Despite the gargantuan amount of liquid he's just consumed, he feels no inclination whatsoever to take a leak. *What the hell am I gonna do?*

Don Carey emerges from the bathroom proudly holding his cup in front of him. "Hey, Chad."

"Don, you got any extra?"

Carey and the drug guy laugh.

"I'm serious," Chad says.

"Go on in," druggie says.

Chad walks very slowly into the bathroom.

Damn it, I don't have to piss at all.

Seated on a stool, facing the toilet, is drug guy number two. He's got a narc's crew cut and a grim expression on his face. His job requires that he *not* wear a suit. He hands Chad a plastic cup.

"Go ahead," the guy says.

Chad glares at him.

"I gotta watch you," the guy explains. "Gotta make sure it's yours."

Chad rolls his eyes. OK, so he was wrong. *This* is the worst job in the world.

"I may have a situation," Chad says, fumbling with his zipper.

"Oh, yeah?"

"I forgot about the test and I peed in the middle of the night."

The drug guy shrugs. "Could be a problem. I don't know."

"I don't know, either," says Chad.

The drug guy nods at Chad's zipper.

Chad unzips his fly and stands, hanging there, over the toilet, the drug guy's nose an inch away. Neither moves. Neither speaks. Hell, what can you say at a time like this? The two men stay frozen in this absurd tableau for what Chad feels, safely, is an eternity.

"I told you," Chad says finally.

"Give it a minute."

Chad lets out a whoosh of breath, scratches his face. Narc taps the top of the toilet bowl.

"So how about those Rams?"

Chad can't believe this. The guy's trying to make small talk.

"I'm from Saint Louis," he explains.

"Nice city."

"Born and raised."

Chad nods.

"Jiggle it," the drug guy says helpfully.

"I ain't a well handle," Chad reminds him.

"Have you had anything to drink since?"

"Oh, yeah. Water, coffee, juice. . . ."

The drug guy abruptly stands and goes over to the sink. He turns on the cold water full blast, then reaches over and flicks on the faucet in the tub. Water rumbles down, splashes into the basin.

But there's no water from Chad. Not even a trickle.

Then, magically, the slightest of tingles, a welcome twitching, and suddenly, without warning, the dam bursts, and the blessed river flows.

Ahhhh. What *relief.* But the relief comes mostly from the awareness that the drug test is about to be over and he can get the hell out of there. Chad pees; the drug guy nods. It might be the worst job in the world, but at least the guy knew what to do in a crisis.

"Amazing," Chad says respectfully.

"Hey." The drug guy shrugs. "I'm a professional."

Monday morning, nine o'clock, at breakfast, Chad shares the drug test story with the rest of the crew. He didn't intend to. Don Carey, who's sitting next to him at the table, peers over his *USA Today,* and says, "Hey, Chad, what took you so long up there?"

Chad clears his throat and begins to explain, quietly, out of earshot of the rest of the dining room and hopefully out of earshot of the rest of the crew. But newspapers drop, and ears cock in his direction as if he's giving a hot stock tip. Leaving out most of the gory details, he tells them what happened. The crew cracks up. When they've calmed down, Hochuli gets them going again by offering Chad his cup of coffee. Chad roars. When he loses it like this in a laugh, he cackles uncontrollably through clenched teeth. Other guests in the dining room start noticing them.

"OK, guys, all right," Hochuli cautions. "Remember, we're NFL officials. Let's act like the pros we are."

A moment of silence.

Then they lose it again. Tears pour from Chad's eyes. Finally, he blurts out, "Please, cut it out, you're gonna make me piss."

"Call the drug guys," Hochuli says.

Chad stands and steadies himself against the table.

"Oh, man," he finally manages as the crew wheezes to a stop. At last. The laughter is a welcome release and

an unexpected extra bond for the weekend. This is
Chad's first year on Ed Hochuli's crew, after six years
with Jerry Markbreit. There have been adjustments to
make, new relationships to forge. In truth, these men are
not exactly his friends. They are, though, in some ways,
closer. It's as if they're a kind of family, bound not by
blood, but by the intimacy that comes with experiencing
something unique, every week, known only to them.
Chad has never spent more intense, concentrated time
with any group of men before. Beyond the camaraderie,
there is, among them all, sincere mutual respect and
trust. At times it feels like they are in a platoon sharing
a foxhole before a crucial battle.

After breakfast, the crew retires to a hotel conference
room reserved for them. The table is set up as it would
be for any business meeting. Legal pads are laid out in
front of each chair, a black Uniball pen grazes the right
corner of each pad, an empty water glass is stationed at
the left corner, cups of sharpened no. 2 pencils are at
strategic easy-to-reach intervals throughout the table.
Two pitchers of water are placed in the center of the
table, lording over a stack of energy bars. A TV monitor
glows catty-corner in the room. A remote control and
videotape cover the top of one of the legal pads. This is
command central, Hochuli's spot, where he'll run the
upcoming five-hour show.

Chad, Ed, and the five other crew members enter the
room. Already seated is Jack Reader, former NFL referee, currently an NFL officials' observer, assigned to Hochuli's crew this week. Reader pumps Hochuli's hand,
congratulates him on the excellent season he and the rest
of his crew are having. Hochuli smiles modestly, chants
a cliché about it being a team effort. Reader grins back.
Hochuli has said exactly the right thing, which was expected. In officials' lingo, Hochuli is well liked in New
York. Chad calls him, respectfully, the golden boy. Ho-

chuli, in addition to having a solid command of both the rules and his crew, has an obvious presence on camera that few referees have shown before. He is reminiscent of the legendary Red Cashion, who virtually demanded camera time by his signature roar, "Firrst *DOWWN!*" Like Cashion, Hochuli has charisma. It's a natural presence, almost a star quality. If Hollywood were doing the Ed Hochuli story, the ideal choice to play him would be George Clooney. The league, hardly naïve to show business, knows it. Hochuli has already earned one Super Bowl, and as long as his grades hold up, there are more where that came from. Chad would love to be there with him.

The crew finds seats. A few fill their water glasses. Briefcases click open, and the tools of the trade, the weekly exams and rule books, emerge. Reading glasses and bifocals plop onto yellow pads. In contrast to the uproarious breakfast, in here it's all business. Hochuli, by trade a partner in a hugely successful Phoenix law firm, is used to conducting serious meetings in conference rooms like this one. There is a strict agenda. The atmosphere is close to that of a graduate school seminar, with Hochuli the professor, Reader the teaching assistant, and the rest of the crew students en route to graduate degrees in NFL officiating.

First order of business, from 10:00 to 11:00, is the review of the test. Hochuli has preselected a few of the trickier test questions for review and discussion.

"What did you get on number fourteen, Bill?" he asks Spyksma.

"True," says Spyksma.

"Why?"

"Because the ball has to go back to the *original* line of scrimmage."

"Yeah, but *why?*"

Morelli offers an explanation. Fincken questions it,

bringing up a call that occurred in a game last year. Carey adds a piece of missing information. In the middle of it all, steering the study session, *refereeing* it, in fact, is Hochuli. Everyone participates. Everybody has done his homework. There is no bullshit, no side trips. Nobody acts the fool; there is no class clown. Someone passing by, unaware of who these seven men sitting around the conference table were, might easily guess CEOs on retreat discussing the future of the world's economy, rather than grown men arguing the rules of a game.

At 11:00, the test picked over clean, its carcass packed away in his briefcase, Chad takes advantage of the five-minute break Hochuli offers while Morelli pops in the training tape. He needs to stretch his legs. Outside the conference room, he joins Don Carey. The two officials hold up the wall.

"Tough test this week," Carey says.

"Yeah, it was. Hell, they're all pretty tough," Chad says.

Carey sighs. Of all the men on this crew, Chad feels the closest to Carey. He's known Don since he was a referee in the Big West, nearly eight years ago. Morelli calls them back inside.

Chad places a friendly hand on Carey's shoulder, saying, "Let's go," but Carey spins away like a lineman rushing a quarterback and is already halfway to his seat.

The crew settles in for the second phase of the weekly meeting—Monday Afternoon at the Movies. For the next three hours, Hochuli rewinds, fast-forwards, pauses, and zooms in on penalty flags, mechanics, and positioning as the crew studies last week's game on tape. It's been a misconception for years that the officials scout the two teams in the game they are about to work, focusing on the players who play hard and fast with the rules. Chad laughs when he hears this. It is completely

inaccurate. Officials view only the last game they
worked. These training sessions, led by each crew's referee, are lessons learned by studying their success and
their mistakes. If they were to watch film of players they
are about to police, they would set themselves up for the
official's curse, the curse of anticipation. Anticipation is,
of course, a good thing if you are an opposing player or
coach. ("See, when the guard rocks forward, it's a
sweep. Look for that. *Anticipate* that.") But anticipation
is heinous for an official. You can never guess. You've
got to *see*.

Notice the left guard. When the guard rocks forward,
he almost always holds. See? You might as well drop
your flag right now, because he's probably going to hold.
Chances are you'll be right. . . .

"Kid," Markbreit always said to Chad, "when you
drop a flag, the penalty better *be* there."

At 4:45, a three-car motorcade leaves the Logan Airport
Ramada Inn and heads down I–93 South toward Foxboro, Mass. The seven men in the cars are all dressed
eerily alike in dark turtlenecks and sport jackets beneath
London Fog topcoats. They all wear Will Smith wrap-
around sunglasses. They look like models on their way
to a *GQ* photo shoot. You would never guess these men
were the NFL officiating crew heading down the pike to
work the ABC Monday Night Football game. They look
too trim, too focused, too *cool*.

Chad rides shotgun with Don Carey at the wheel,
Tom Fincken in the back. On the ride in, Chad is stonily
quiet. He likes to use the drive into the stadium as prep
time, time to get himself mentally ready for the game
he's about to officiate. He tries to clear his mind and
remind himself of certain mechanics. His mantra goes:
*Move toward the line of scrimmage, keep your eyes out
of the backfield, don't anticipate.* By this point in the

season, the eleventh game, Carey and Fincken know the drive in is Chad's time and don't bother talking to him. They leave him looking out the window, absently fingering the glass, in his own world.

An hour later, the motorcade pulls into the parking lot at Foxboro Stadium and crawls toward the players' entrance. Two NFL security guards wearing blue windbreakers and holding walkie-talkies wave them to slanted parking places next to the team buses. Hochuli bounds out of the lead car, grins at the security guards.

"Hey, guys."

"Ha ya doin'?" A chowder-thick Boston accent cuts the crisp late-afternoon air. It's just after five and it's almost dark. *Jesus,* thinks Chad, *this is like being in a foreign country or on Mars.*

The second security guard gestures at them with his radio. "Lawk up yeh cehs and folla me." His accent is worse than the first guy's. The caravan of officials walks toward the players' gate.

"Imagine talking like that?" Carey whispers to Chad.

"You do," Chad shoots back. Carey laughs.

In order to get to the officials' locker room in Foxboro Stadium, you have to walk onto the field first. The locker room itself is the worst in the league. Calling it a pit would be giving it an upgrade. It's barely the size of a broom closet that manages, somehow, to extend to two levels. Two lousy levels. The shower is on the upper level, a true pain in the ass if your locker is on the bottom level. As Chad enters the locker room and surveys the surroundings, he thinks, *If this were a prison, we'd riot. Oh, well. In a couple of years the Patriots will be moving to a brand-new stadium closer to the city. They ought to let us design the officials' locker room in the new place.*

Now begins the game prep. First order of business: cast and injury report. Chad heads over to each team's locker room, a lot more spacious and luxurious than the officials', and visits with the trainer from each team. Each trainer hands him a white index-sized card on which the trainer has filled in the date, the team and the players, numbers only, who are wearing protective casts and on which body part.

Chad makes small talk with each trainer, collects the cast report cards, and waits while each man scratches his signature at the bottom. There are no players wearing casts in this game.

Next assignment: equipment check. Chad finds each team's equipment manager and asks if there are players wearing anything unusual for tonight's game. In reality, this is a routine visor check, to see which players, if any, will be wearing clear or tinted visors. No one on the Dolphins has a visor. On New England, wide receiver Terry Glenn and linebacker Henry Thomas are scheduled to wear clear visors. Chad wonders why the league doesn't just call this a visor check. What other kind of unusual equipment would a player be wearing? A head cam? Removable dread locks? Eyebrow pins? A tongue ring?

Last, Chad checks with the special teams' coaches to record the uniform numbers of players who are eligible to be "flyers," wing players who race downfield to cover kickoffs and punts.

By the time Chad returns to the locker room, the rest of the crew are dressed in their uniforms. Chad dresses slowly, reflectively, doing a mental checklist, making sure he hasn't forgotten any of his pregame responsibilities. Before he slips on his stripes, he presses both hands against the wall, leans one leg straight back, and begins ten minutes of serious stretching.

"TV's here," announces Don Carey.

Chad slowly rises. "How you doin'?" he asks rhetorically. Two members of the ABC television technical crew walk into the locker room. The first man, older, a warm smile, is familiar. The second man is tall, narrow, all Adam's apple, and brand-new.

"Nice digs," the older one says to Chad.

"Yeah. I'm thinking of taking my wife here for our anniversary."

"Officials always get shitboxes, I don't know why," Older says to Adam's apple.

"We get no respect, that's why," Chad says. He reflexively raises both arms. Older leans over, attaches a wire and a microphone switch around Chad's waist, and clips a tiny microphone to the front of his shirt.

"We mike the umpire," Older explains to Adam's apple, "so the television audience can hear the snap count. You know, hut-hut-hut!"

"And so the people at home can hear the thump-thump-*thump* sound in the meat grinder," adds Chad.

"Meat grinder?" Adam's apple peers up at Chad.

"I'll explain it to you when you're older," Older says.

About thirty minutes before kickoff, as the Dolphins and Patriots warm up on the field, Chad stands on the fifty-yard line with Tom Fincken, the side judge, and Ken Deininger, a team representative for the New England Patriots. Included in Deininger's job description is meeting with the umpire and side judge before each home game to peruse all 100 players on the field and note any uniform violations. Chad holds another white index-sized card, marked "Game Day Uniform Violations," a pencil at the ready.

"See anything?"

"Eighty-seven. Ben Coates," says Deininger. "Look at his socks."

Fincken grunts agreement. "Down by his ankles."

Chad nods, jots down: "Coates, 87, socks."

"There's another one. Thirty-three."

"Yep," says Chad. "Karim Abdul-Jabbar. Socks." He adds Abdul-Jabbar's name to the card.

"Zack Thomas. What's up with your pants?"

Fincken points to the Miami linebacker. He's lying on the field, stretching. His pants are a foot above his knees.

"Fashion statement," says Deininger.

"Looks like he's wearing culottes," says Chad, writing Thomas's name below Abdul-Jabbar's.

Chad knows that, for the most part, the uniform check during warm-ups is merely an exercise. These players guilty of uniform violations now will come out of their locker rooms for the game properly dressed. They know that the National Football League enforces its strict uniform policy by assessing stiff fines. Chad's not crazy about the duty, but as an umpire one of his responsibilities is, simply, to police clothes.

The way players feel about uniform violations is the same way most of us feel about speed traps: pissed off and convinced that there are better ways for the police to spend their time. An example of this occurred several years ago before the then Los Angeles Raiders–Denver Broncos game. Art Shell was the coach of the Raiders, and Marcus Allen was his star player. For almost the entire season the league had been pressuring the umpires to slap Marcus Allen with a uniform violation. He was defying the league dress code by wearing his pants well above his knees.

Chad stood at the fifty during warm-ups, eyes glued on Marcus. Sure enough, Allen's pants were a foot above his knees. Chad scribbled Allen's number down on his violations card and waited for the Raiders to return to their locker room.

A few minutes later, Chad came into the locker room. Art Shell greeted him.

"Hey, Chad, what's up?"

"What's up? Marcus's pants. I want to talk to both of you."

"No way. That's really why you're here?"

"You got it," said Chad. "I'm the fashion police."

"Fine, good, talk to him. He's been wearing his pants up all year. Thinks it makes him harder to tackle."

"He's in violation, Art."

"I know that. I tell him to put 'em right every game. Maybe he'll listen to you. He sure won't listen to me."

Chad found Marcus sitting in front of his locker, smearing his trademark black eye goo beneath each eye.

"Hey, Marcus."

"Chad Brown. Now this is an honor, having the umpire visit me before the game, *personally*."

"Yeah, well, I'm here on league business. It's about your pants."

"Oh, come on. Not that shit again."

"I don't make the rules, Marcus. You can wear your pants on your head for all I care. But the league says you have to bring 'em down, below your knees, or they're gonna fine you. Big-time."

Marcus Allen took a moment to consider this. Then he went crazy: "This is really why they sent you in here? To bust my balls about my *pants*? I don't believe this shit! How much are they paying you to come in here and hassle me while I'm trying to prepare for the game? *Huh*? Don't you have something more important to do?"

Chad looked at him and shrugged. "It's really simple, Marcus. Lower your pants or pay the fine."

Marcus slammed his locker shut. The clang of the door startled Chad for a second. It echoed in his head as he got up and left.

On his way out of the locker room, he passed Art Shell. The coach looked at Chad sympathetically.

"Well? How'd it go?"

"Great. We're going out to dinner later."

"I bet."

Chad sighed and stepped onto the field. "Damn sensitive about his pants," he mumbled to himself.

He grinned as he remembered the Marcus Allen incident. He sees Marcus regularly these days. He's an analyst with FOX-TV. The first time Chad saw him this year was on the sidelines before the San Diego–San Francisco preseason game. With a grave expression on his face, Chad approached Marcus and, without saying a word, bent down and picked up Allen's pants cuffs.

"You're all right," Chad said, and continued right past him.

Marcus was too startled to reply.

Now, a few minutes before *Monday Night Football,* Chad begins his final pregame duty, the always-popular foreign substance check. Once again, he pulls out a white index-sized card and his trusty pencil. Four linemen—two Dolphins and two Patriots—stand waiting impatiently in the mouth of the tunnel. Chad greets them hastily and starts patting down their jerseys, seeking, in vain, any substance that isn't kosher concealed somewhere within the folds of the twelve hundred pounds of beef looming in front of him. Satisfied they're all clean, he dismisses them. Out of the corner of his eye he sees them rumble back toward their teams as he completes his last pregame card of the day and waits for the game to begin.

At that moment, Chad is transported back in time, to that day in Denver when he told Marcus Allen to adjust his uniform or pay a fine. No one was more surprised than Chad when Marcus Allen raced through the tunnel with the rest of the Raiders and lined up for the national anthem, his pants well below his knees, in full compliance with the league.

Marcus caught Chad's eye. He pointed a finger at the umpire, then down at his pants. Chad smiled and nodded.

Well, thought Chad, *I guess they do listen to me.*

FOURTH QUARTER
VI

13
THE GOOD, THE BAD,
AND THE UGLY

Chad turns and catches Kevin Greene staring at him. The Pro Bowl linebacker and one of the most intense players in the league grinds his teeth as if he's Hannibal Lecter and Chad is lunch.

"How you doin'?" Chad asks. "Everything OK?"

Greene turns away, says nothing. Gets his head back into the game. Greene begins each game at insane, then builds from there.

Ty Detmer starts the second half with a pass. Incomplete. Second and ten. Garrison Hearst shoots up the middle. Nothing. Jim Fox, Carolina's 300-pound nose tackle, stuffs him, making a weird animal sound, "Aghhrr!"

Chad runs over, taps Fox on the butt, tells him to let Hearst up. "Play's over, big man, play's over."

"Aghhrr!" Fox hops off Hearst like he's playing horsey with one of his kids and lumbers away.

Third and ten. Detmer drops back. Chad charges the line of scrimmage, but his eyes are nowhere near the backfield. He looks right at Gogan. Kevin, groaning and pushing, puts all of his weight, all 350 pounds, into Sean Gilbert's chest. Gilbert, well over three hundred pounds himself, is stood straight up by Gogan. Gogan's face turns a deep purple, the color of an eggplant, as he endures a continuous flurry of whacks and slaps from Gilbert, never relinquishing his block. Behind him, Detmer releases a bomb toward Jerry Rice.

Rice, no longer the speed burner he once was but still smooth as silk, cuts like an arrow toward the left sideline. The ball falls into his arms like a baby. Chad whirls to watch. Rice tiptoes out-of-bounds as George Hayward brings both arms down emphatically to signal it's a good catch. Rice, implacable, flips the ball to Chad as he runs by.

"Nice catch, Jerry," Chad says.

Oops. That was a no-no. An official is never supposed to compliment a player. According to an archaic unwritten code among officials, a compliment suggests favoritism and, therefore, interferes with impartiality. Chad doesn't agree. If someone does something special on the field or plays a strong game overall, Chad tells him. Actually, he can't help it. It's the fan inside him coming out.

"You've got to suppress that fan inside you," Jerry Markbreit has warned him a thousand times.

"I try," Chad insists.

He just can't help it.

"Great game," he once said to Bart Oates, center on the Super Bowl champion New York Giants, after a tough game against the Cowboys. In a postgame interview, a member of the media congratulated Oates on having an outstanding game.

"Thanks," said Oates. "I thought I had a pretty good game, too. In fact, one of the officials told me I played a great game, said I blocked my ass off."

Oates's quote appeared in the New York newspapers the next day. Jerry Seeman went through the roof and, miffed, called Markbreit.

"Tell your crew not to congratulate players, for crissakes," he warned Markbreit.

"Was that you?" Markbreit asked Chad later.

"Hell, no," Chad lied.

In his mind, as long as he is paid to be an official, Chad will be, first and foremost, completely impartial. But in his heart, as long as he is alive, he will be, first and foremost, a football fan.

The partisan 'Frisco crowd is ignited after Rice's catch. Chad spots the ball on the Carolina thirty. The 49ers have come out fired up. Detmer drops back one step, lines a laser to Terrell Owens, who fights his way down to the eight-yard line. First and goal.

Chad is caught up in the drive. The play has been fast and fierce, but there are no flags. Gogan points a finger at him. Chad looks away.

The Niners give the ball to Hearst. He blasts down to the four. Second and goal. Then Irv Smith, the reserve tight end, dashes into the huddle with a play. Chad senses something.

The 49ers break their huddle. Their formation appears normal enough. Two running backs. A wideout. But Chad looks carefully. One of the running backs is Jerry Rice. Kevin Greene sees this at the same time.

"Rice is in the backfield! Who's got him?"

Nobody knows who should cover Rice, so everybody does.

Chad smiles. He knows that Rice is just a decoy. Chad watches as Detmer's pass sails toward the corner of the end zone, nowhere near Rice, but right into the awaiting arms of Terrell Owens. Touchdown! This time Owens does a legitimate victory dance. A little leg waggle, a touch of head swivel, a smidgen of Dirty Bird. The extra point is good. Carolina 16, 49ers 14.

Don Carey, the back judge, and Pete Morelli, the field judge, both of whom gave the touchdown signal, approach Chad during the time-out before the kickoff.

"That was all cool, right, Chad?"

"Yeah. The formation was cool. And I didn't see anything. This is a pretty clean game."

"To tell you the truth," says Carey, "I was faked out. I was looking at Rice and Owens got behind me."

"You were lucky," Chad says.

The teams prepare for the kickoff. This game is a surprise. Carolina came in as a twelve-point underdog. Bates returns the kickoff to the Carolina thirty-five. The 49er defense, led by Norton, knows they have to make a statement, right here, right now. They blitz. Beuerlein throws incomplete. Fred Lane runs for seven behind a block by Floyd. Then Lane takes a pitch from Beuerlein and goes for twenty yards. Hochuli throws a flag.

"Hold. Number 56. Offense. Repeat third down."

Dom Capers, the Carolina coach, goes insane. He rips off his headset and stalks Hochuli as the referee marks off the ten-yard penalty.

"Are you nuts, Ed? That was a good block! What are you doing to us here? For crissakes, they don't need your help!"

Chad runs over and pulls Hochuli away.

"You got something, Chad?"

"No. Just walk away."

Third down. Beuerlein throws to Muhammad, who drops the ball. As it so frequently does, the penalty has stopped the drive.

Carolina punts.

Chad knows he's got to watch the run. The Niners are going to keep running Garrison Hearst behind Gogan and see if he can chew up the Carolina defense. Sure enough, Hearst runs up Gogan's back for eight yards. Gogan is now playing purple, grunting and grinding on every play, looking for people to hit. On second down, Gogan blasts John Brady, the middle linebacker, and Hearst gallops for five more yards and a first down. The ball rests on the Carolina thirty-five.

Chad feels it. Play action. After a short count, Detmer fakes to Hearst and goes back to pass. He sees Rice open in the middle. His arm starts to come forward, just as he's slammed into from behind. The ball flies out of his hand. Les Miller, a second-string Carolina lineman, scoops it up and rumbles upfield. Chad chases the play. After about fifteen yards, Miller's knees start to buckle. He sucks in some air, and then he crumbles. He struggles back to his feet and is tapped on the butt by J. J. Stokes.

Chad, right on top of the play, does absolutely nothing.

Which is exactly what he should do.

Miller, in a complete fog, looks desperately at Chad for help. *Am I down? Should I keep running? What the hell is going on?*

He who hesitates is tackled.

Four 49ers climb onto Miller like a play structure and pull him to the ground. Terrell Owens sneaks his sure hands around the football and yanks it out of Miller's midsection. He turns and sprints the other way. Chad reverses direction and follows Owens down the sideline, where, trying to avoid Kevin Greene's lunge, he steps out-of-bounds.

Then, for the first time in a year, Chad Brown blows his whistle.

The crowd is confused. The players are confused. The coaches are confused. But Ed Hochuli is decisive. He faces the television camera and announces emphatically, "After the ball was fumbled, the Carolina player was down by contact. It's Carolina ball. First down!"

Unfortunately, Hochuli is also wrong.

On the sideline, Steve Mariucci literally starts jumping up and down. "*What?* Ed! He wasn't touched!"

Chad rests his hand gently on Mariucci's arm. "I got it, Steve, I got it."

He runs over to Hochuli. "Ed, that's not what I saw."

"No? Then what . . . ?"

"He wasn't down by contact. He was touched after he picked up the ball. I blew the whistle when Owens stepped out-of-bounds. It's 49er ball."

"Jesus. Are you sure?"

"Positive."

Hochuli hesitates.

"I'm going with you, Chad," he says finally. "I've got to reverse myself. Christ. Capers is gonna have a fit."

"It's the right call, Ed."

Hochuli nods. He sighs, then snaps on his mike and announces that he was wrong. It's 49er ball, after all.

On the field, Dom Capers is going ballistic. Wins are hard for his team to come by. And losses cost jobs. He charges Hochuli. Hochuli knows he's got to give Capers his day in court.

"You're killing me, Ed! He was down, goddammit! This is such bullshit!" He throws up his hands and walks away.

"Chad was on it, Dom," Hochuli shouts after him. "It's the right call."

It's not about who wins or loses.

It's about making the right call. Making sure both teams play by the rules.

"I'm obsessed with that," says Chad. "Obsessed with making the right call. It's what keeps me going and what keeps me up at night. I lie awake some nights watching my own personal *ESPN SportsCenter* in my head. I replay the highlights of the week, the good calls I made. Then I'll throw in the bad calls, too, just to keep me honest. Once in a while, I'll do the 'The Best of Chad Brown,' a trip down memory lane, and screen the good, the bad, and the ugly over my seven years in the National Football League.

"I've had some beauts. . . ."

Philadelphia Eagles–San Francisco 49ers. 1995.

As far as Chad is concerned, William "The Refrigerator" Perry has no business being on the punt return team. As he moves his massive frame, all nine thousand pounds of him, or whatever the freight car scale says he weighs, onto the gridiron, Chad is tempted to drop a flag and penalize the Eagles for having an extra man on the field. *I guess I shouldn't second-guess Buddy Ryan, though. The Eagles are off to their hottest start in decades, something like 9–0. If Buddy wants to put him on special teams, fine. Fridge himself is the size of a four-man wedge.*

The center snaps the ball. It rockets off the punter's toe and spirals like a shot into the sky, eventually landing into the blue-gloved basket of the return man. He bolts upfield. Bodies fly, then crash into each other. Right in front of him, in what seems like super slow motion, Chad sees a taped hand reach straight up, latch onto a face mask, twist, and *yank*. He launches his yellow handkerchief into the air. It's an obvious call. A no-brainer. Except for one little thing.

Chad doesn't have the offender's number.

And in Jerry Markbreit's book, no number, no foul.

But this is such a blatant infraction. Dangerously close to a personal foul.

Jerry puts a parental arm on Chad's shoulder. "What do you got?"

"I got a foul, Jerry. A face mask. But I don't have the number."

"What do you mean, you don't have the number?"

"What I mean is, I don't have the *number*."

"I have it."

Chad and Markbreit look up. Fridge is thundering past them on his way to the bench. His stomach undulates like the Pacific Ocean during a tsunami.

"Huh?" says Markbreit.

"I know who it was."

"Wait a minute." Markbreit hustles over to him. "Tell me who it was."

Fridge stops, considers the small white-capped man in the striped shirt so far below him.

"Why should I tell you?" he sniffs.

Right now, there's only one thing Fridge is going to give Markbreit: shade.

"Fridge," is all Chad says.

"Oh, all right, I'll tell you. Number 85."

And then he whispers to Chad, "You owe me a steak."

Seattle Seahawks–San Diego Chargers. 1996.

When I turn on SportsCenter, thought Chad Brown, *the last person I want to see is* me.

But there I am, big as life, Chris Berman and Tom Jackson doing a number on me, giving me a taste of prime time like I'm Deion Sanders or Reggie White.

Of course, the only reason they're talking about me is that I screwed up. That's the only way an official ever gets on ESPN. That or if he happened to die on the field.

Late in the first half, the Seahawks are moving, driving toward the end zone. They've got the ball on the San Diego twelve-yard line. The offense breaks the huddle, lines up. The Seattle quarterback drops back to pass. Chad moves toward the line of scrimmage and sees the right guard grab a fistful of the defensive end's jersey, twist, and slam him down into the turf. We call that holding. Definitely. Hand to the belt. The yellow flag soars.

But.

In that moment, as the flag flies, in sudden super slow motion, there is *doubt*. In the back of his mind there is a nagging feeling, like a sting from a mosquito bite. Suddenly Chad remembers good old Howie Long, and a question drills its way into his skull: *Is that a hold . . . or is it a rip?*

Meanwhile, in the end zone, there is celebration. Joey Galloway high-steps like he's in the Grambling marching band, then he stops and tomahawk-spikes the football into the ground. In Seattle, there is dancing in the aisles.

On the field, however, there is yellow laundry.

Jerry looks at Chad. Chad looks at Jerry. Jerry tilts his head and scrunches his mouth up ever so slightly.

He's giving me that look, thinks Chad. The Jerry Look Number One. The this-better-be-a-good-call-Chad look.

"What ya got, Chad?"

"Jerry, I think I've got a flag for holding."

"You *think*?"

"Yeah. Because it could've been a rip."

Now here comes Jerry Look Number Two. The this-call-is-your-call-Chad-even-though-I'm-the-referee-because-you-dropped-a-flag-and-you-really-aren't-sure-and-everyone-in-the-immediate-world-is-watching-us-so-hurry-up-look.

"I'm not sure," says Chad. "So I want to pick up the flag."

"Are you *sure*?"

"I'm sure," Chad says, then clarifies, "about picking it up."

"Then pick it up," Jerry says.

Chad stuffs the handkerchief back into his belt just as Jerry announces to the Seahawks, Chargers, and rest of the world, "There was no flag on the play. The touchdown stands."

Adults express anger and frustration in various ways. They may scream, shout, swear, stomp, threaten, throw things, or even throw tantrums.

Bobby Ross, head coach of the San Diego Chargers, is unique because he does *all* of the above.

He begins with a simple Zen-like stare. For the briefest moment, it appears as if he's putting himself in a trance, meditating. Don't be fooled. His mouth is about to open and the furies inside him are about to come spewing out.

"What the *HELL ARE YOU DOING?* You're *PICKING UP THAT FLAG?* You can't do that! *DO YOU HEAR MEEEE?* That is the *WORST CALL I'VE EVER SEEN!* You are blind! You are *innnCOMPETENT*! Worse than that, you *STINK*! This is the worst officiating *EVER*!"

"Wow," says Chad.

"He'll cool off," promises Jerry. "Just ignore him."

Chad glances at the sideline. It's hard to ignore a man who's just ripped off his headset and is kicking the Gatorade bucket. Mercifully, there is a television time-out. Ross stomps onto the field and waves at Jerry as if he's guiding a plane in for a landing.

"Jerry! Comere! I want to talk to you!"

Another Jerry look. Jerry Look Number Three. The I-got-a-migraine-feels-like-my-head's-gonna-explode look.

"Don't look at me," Chad says. "He's talking to you."

Jerry hitches up his pants and joins Bobby Ross on the sideline. Jerry nods sympathetically while Ross rages. After a final nod, Jerry jogs back toward Chad.

"I guess you really told him."

"Yeah. Now he wants to talk to you."

"*Me?* Why me?"

"Must be your lucky day."

Chad doesn't even reach the sideline before Bobby Ross is right *in* his face.

"That call!" he fumes. "That was *horrible*! Terrible! The worst I've ever seen. You hear me? *The worst!* That was the worst call in *THE HISTORY OF THIS NATIONAL FOOTBALL LEAGUE*!"

And now for the moment that appeared on national television. Chad's fifteen seconds of fame. Or infamy.

Chad walks down the sideline, trying to get away from Bobby Ross. But Ross is on a mission. He's out to bag an umpire. He chases Chad, catches up to him, and wags his finger in his face. "It's Sunday afternoon, Chad Brown!" he screams. "I'm gonna make a phone call, and when I get through with you, you will not be working in this league by tomorrow morning! You hear me! You will not be working in the National Football League by Monday morning! *YOU HEAR ME?*"

It's days like this, ponders Chad as he watches ESPN SportsCenter, *that I wish I never got cable.*

San Francisco 49ers–Miami Dolphins. 1995.

There comes a time, in every umpire's life, when he must leave home and venture forth, out of the meat grinder. It's healthy. Umpires learn that there's a whole new world out there. A world beyond the discordant blood and bone of six three-hundred–pound leviathans pounding one another into the ground like croquet hoops. A quieter world, more subdued, a world of smooth, lithe linebackers and speedy, sinewy corners shadowing balletic wide receivers. It's so much more civilized out there.

Right.

Chad realizes immediately that it's going to be a pass. Marino throws a million of them, and he telegraphs each one. *Concentrate*, Chad reminds himself. *Charge the line of scrimmage, watch my guys, the center and guards, see anything? Nope. Nothing there. Now turn and watch the flight of the ball.* Once a game, maybe, Chad will have to make a call on a pass. It's certainly not going to be *this* pass. This is a forty-yard bomb, and both the head linesman and side judge are right there, practically *wearing* both the wideout and the cover man.

It's amazing, then, that they don't see the foul.

It's right in front of them.

As the wide receiver reaches for the football, the defensive back grabs his face mask. Both men explode onto the sideline, disappearing into a cloud of white chalk. Chad waits for the flag to be dropped. The head linesman and the side judge make eye contact. Clearly, their vision has been blocked by both players. Because neither official reaches into his belt.

Chad, forty yards away, doesn't hesitate. With the speed of a gunslinger, he draws his flag. He winds up and throws it as far as he can. He gets almost as much distance as Marino. *I guess all my weight training finally paid off*, Chad thinks as his flag lands with a thud at the head linesman's feet.

"Good call."

Markbreit is right behind him.

"I might be forty yards away, but I'm one hundred percent sure of this one," says Chad.

"Hey, kid," Jerry says as they hustle upfield, "if you hadn't thrown it, I was going to throw it. I just would've thrown it a little farther, that's all."

Kansas City Chiefs–San Diego Chargers. 1994.

Lee "Hacksaw" Hamilton is a Southern California legend. Holding court on sports talk radio's golden hours, the prestigious afternoon drive-time shift from 4:00 until 7:00 on AM 690 in San Diego, Hamilton calls himself, immodestly, the Franchise. In 1994, Hacksaw was also the play-by-play announcer for the San Diego Chargers, a screaming, craggy-voiced homer. When things went the Chargers' way, he invited Sunday's star on his talk show. When the Chargers suffered a loss, which was often, he offered a forum for a carefully chosen goat or victim or Bobby Ross, the head coach, who was usually both.

One Monday afternoon, following a Sunday defeat to the Kansas City Chiefs, Hacksaw is hosting Harry Swayne, the Chargers' giant offensive tackle, who wants his day in court. On Sunday, Swayne felt he had been wronged, falsely and unfairly accused, and he wants to prove his innocence.

"Before we bang phone calls, Harry, tell us," croaks Hamilton. "How bad was that call?"

"Hacksaw, I don't want to get upset. I don't want to start throwing furniture in here or bust a wall or anything, but that was, without a doubt, the worst call I've ever had against me. Forget that. That was the worst call I've ever *seen*. No way in the world I was holding. No *way*. That umpire was blind."

"I have to agree with you, Harry. From where I was sitting, twenty rows up in the broadcast booth, I'd say you were holding on that play about as much as I was."

"You got that right, Hacksaw. The way we're going, we sure don't need any extra help from the officials."

"Agreed again. What do *you* think, Southern California? I wanna know. Call me, Lee 'Hacksaw' Hamilton, and talk to me. And talk to Harry Swayne of *your* San Diego Chargers. What was that official's name again, Harry?"

"It was the umpire. I know him, too. Damn. What is his *name*?"

"Chad Brown," Chad says aloud to the radio. He's driving home, down the 405, listening to Hacksaw on the Mighty Six Ninety, one of life's simple pleasures, until now. He replays the moment. . . .

Late in the third quarter. Kansas City pins San Diego back to their two-yard line. On the first play from scrimmage, the Charger quarterback fades back and uncorks a bomb. The Charger wideout curls beneath it, high-steps out of the defensive back's grasp, and sprints the length of the field for a ninety-eight-yard touchdown. Brilliant play, perfect pass, marvelous catch and run. There's only one hitch.

There's a yellow flag bunched up on the ground. Chad's.

"What did you see?" Jerry asks him.

"Pull-down."

"Holding. Man, after a play like that."

"I saw it, Jerry."

"Give me the number."

"Seventy-four. Harry Swayne."

Jerry grimaces. "He's gonna love this."

"Gonna love me, too."

Jerry waves for the ball, calling the touchdown back. The crowd responds with all the warmth of a lynch mob. Jerry flicks on his mike and this time, keeping his usual flair in check, announces the penalty with the solemnity of a clergyman announcing upcoming funeral services.

"Holding. Number 74. Repeat first down."

Swayne charges toward Chad. "I was not holding! That was a bad call! A horrible call! How can you throw a flag on that play? I tell you, man, I've seen some bad calls, but this one has to be one of the worst! No, I'm wrong, I'm sorry I said that. It was *absolutely* the worst. Nothing comes close."

"Look, Harry, shake it off. You got a whole quarter left. Play the game."

"Play the game. You make playing the game *work*."

Chad pulls into his driveway. It was a tough call, and at the time he felt bad about dropping his flag. He's an official, not a rally killer. The fan inside him hated that he was responsible for reversing that touchdown. There is no worse feeling than making a call that affects the outcome of a game.

He leans back in his seat and massages his forehead. Hacksaw's voice continues to hammer him in the background. Enough. He reaches for the on/off knob.

". . . so, Harry, I'm still stumped. If the call was so obviously wrong, to you, to me, to sixty thousand fans in the stadium and millions more at home, tell me, tell all of Southern California, if there was no holding on that play, why did the umpire drop the flag?"

"I got the answer to that, Hacksaw."

"You do?"

"Oh, yeah. The umpire bet me a six-pack of beer that he would. A six-pack of Amstel light. They a sponsor?"

Chad bolts upright and slams his head into the rear-view mirror. "I bet you a *what?*" he wails.

What a crock! He dissolves backward into his cushy leather seat. He immediately makes a mental list of all the people he has to call, right now, before Swayne's dumb-ass statement hits the media shark tank, although he knows he's already too late: Markbreit, Seeman, each member of his crew, Hacksaw. *Man. Somebody's got to call Hacksaw. It sure as hell isn't going to be me.*

And Swayne.

Can you believe that guy? The next game I work with Swayne . . .

Damn it! Anyone who knows me knows two things about me: First, I'm a man of integrity. I would never, ever, make a bet like that. A six-pack of Amstel light. That is so ridiculous.

Which brings me to the second thing.
Everybody knows I drink Bud.

Southwest Community College–Harbor College.
1987.

OK, so it's not the Super Bowl. And the players aren't
exactly superstars. And to make ends meet the coaches
have to do double duty, teaching courses like Basic
Physical Education or The Art of Public Speaking. And
instead of playing their games in front of fifty thousand
screaming fans, they play in front of dozens of whining
friends and family. Still, the kids play hard and with
pride, and the coaches take their jobs as seriously as
Bobby Ross does. Well, maybe not *that* seriously.

It's late in the game. Southwest owns the football and
is driving toward the Harbor end zone. The Southwest
quarterback, a tricky ball handler who can fake better
than he can throw, drops back to pass. On every pass
his feet shuffle in a hundred different directions as he
scans the field for a receiver. His feet are moving so
much he looks as if he's doing the cha-cha or he has to
take a serious piss. Chad's watching him like a camera.
This is before the Banana and before he learned to keep
his eyes out of the backfield. The quarterback's eyes pop
open. He sees somebody. Yep. Got a receiver, down
there somewhere, near the goal line. One, two, cha cha
cha. Three, four, cha cha cha. Arm goes back. Ball is
released . . .

And Chad blows his whistle.

Just as the ball, fluttering like a dying bird, lands in
the hands of a shocked Harbor College linebacker. He
looks into his midsection, fondles the football. Yep. It's
there. He starts to sprint upfield but abruptly stops. There
was that whistle and you always stop when you hear a

whistle. The kid tosses the ball to the umpire, who looks so dazed he nearly drops it. Guy's got a very weird expression on his face. The Southwest receiver trots back to the quarterback and screams, "How open do I have to be?"

"I know, I know," mumbles the quarterback, who knows he should've had him.

The Harbor linebacker shakes his head, returns to his defense. "I was gone, man. Nothing but empty real estate ahead of me. I was *gone*."

"Long gone. Game over. We win," moans the right tackle and defensive captain.

"Damn," says the linebacker.

"Shake it off. Let's just get the penalty."

"Yeah. What was that whistle?" agrees the quarterback as he joins the assembly of players from both sides.

Chad takes a deep breath.

You hear about this sometimes, but you think it'll never happen to you. You're too good. Too experienced. Too much of a man. *Don't be embarrassed*, he tells himself. *It happens to everyone.*

Not to me, he insists. *It's never happened to me before. Man, this is embarrassing. It's more than that. It's goddamn* humiliating.

Come on, a voice inside his head says. *Just because it happened, it doesn't make you less of an official. It doesn't mean you can't have a good game in other ways. And if you put pressure on yourself, which is what you're doing right now, it could happen again. So just relax. And continue to perform. You must try to overcome the condition known as* . . .

Premature ewhistleation.

Commonly known as the inadvertent whistle.

Described as accidentally blowing your whistle. Or blowing your whistle too soon.

The umpire's nightmare.
Pray that it never happens to you.

Oakland Raiders–Denver Broncos. 1994.

"There are some officials who just don't belong in the
meat grinder," says Chad. "Most of them, actually. All
the wing guys, that's for sure. Even certain umpires, although they work in here, don't *belong* in here. And
referees? I don't think so. They come in here unannoun-
ced, uninvited, all bets are off. They're taking their
chances. I can't be responsible for what might happen.
Even if the referee is my referee, Jerry Markbreit."

First half. Tight game. Elway fakes to the halfback
and pitches out to his fullback, a punishing blocker, a
guy who can stick you, but a guy who has hands made
of stone. The ball ricochets off the two rocks attached
to his wrists and skies high into the air before it slams
onto the ground and rolls crazily toward the end zone.
Everybody on the field gallops after the football. Sto-
nefingers has the lead. He bends over, tries to pick it up,
and *kicks* it ten yards in front of him. Finally, the right
offensive tackle dives on it. His aim's a bit off, because
he totally misses it. He slams into the ground. The ball
squirts away, twirls to the left, zigzagging like a runaway
rabbit toward the end zone.

Two people have a bead on it. Markbreit, who's running at full speed right behind the ball, on top of the
play like the proficient referee he is, and Howie Long,
the huge Raider defensive tackle, who decides that this
ball, this miniature leather torpedo, is his and his alone.
Long, completely focused on the football, doesn't see
Jerry. He grunts and belly flops onto the ball, taking
Markbreit with him. He lands on Jerry with the force of
a building being dynamited. Jerry lies beneath him, buried. alive.

Long hardly notices him. He probably barely *feels* him. With the ball snugly cradled in his arms, Long hustles to his feet and, showing Markbreit all the respect of a floor mat, steps on and across his back, embedding him farther into the ground. With two Broncos dangling from him, Long flings himself forward and picks up another five yards before he's shoved out-of-bounds.

Chad, the trailer, is right on top of the play. He's seen every move of the crazy sequence, highlighted by Jerry's near-death experience beneath Howie Long's bulk. Chad takes over, signals the fumble, marks the spot.

Markbreit scrambles to his feet, hoping that the sixty thousand people present might have missed the fact that he was recently trampled by a rampaging lineman. He casually dusts himself off, trying, as he does, to regain his breath, his composure, and his dignity. Regaining his dignity is especially hard because his face is smudged and streaked with dirt and he's standing on his hat.

"What happened?" he manages to ask as he spits out a mouthful of Mile High turf.

"A fumble."

Chad feels himself starting to go. He chokes back a laugh.

"I know it was a fumble! What I don't know is who the hell ran up my back? That's what I want to know. Who was it? Give me a name."

As he speaks, Jerry retrieves his white referee's cap and puts it on his head. Unseen by him, two clumps of grass hang over the side of the brim. Chad loses it.

"What the hell is so funny?"

"Nothing, Jerry."

"Yeah? I wanna talk to the guy who hit me. Set him straight. Who was it?"

"Him."

Chad points to Howie Long, who's propped up

against a teammate because he's doubled over with laughter.

"It was him," Chad repeats. "Howie Long. Go talk to him, Jerry. I'll go with you."

"Ah, fuck it. He's just lucky I don't go over there and kick his ass."

"Good decision."

"Come on, we got a football game here."

"Yep." Chad tilts his head and grins down at Jerry. *"What?"*

Should I tell him about the two clumps of grass hanging off his hat? Or should I just let him fry?

"Why do you keep staring at me? What are you, nuts? Come on, I wanna get this game in before next *Sukkas*."

Let him fry.

14
THE ALL—CHAD BROWN
ALL—MEAT GRINDER TEAM

The momentum has shifted. You can feel it. With the ball on the Carolina forty-three, Garrison Hearst bangs for seven yards. Then on second down, Gogan flattens Jeff Brady and Hearst bursts through the hole for a big first down at the thirty. Detmer fakes to Hearst and hits Stokes in the back of the end zone. Touchdown. It's now San Francisco 20, Carolina 16. The 49ers decide to go for two. Detmer drills the ball to Owens. The conversion is good. The quarter runs out with the 49ers ahead, 22–16.

During the television time-out, Hochuli comes over to Chad.

"That fumble, that was a weird play. I thought about it and you were absolutely right. Good call."

"Thanks. I thought I was right because he wasn't touched. Then I was *sure*. So I blew my whistle. When's the last time I did that?"

"Not since you've been on my crew."

"How's this? Not since last year."

Hochuli laughs. He doesn't know whether Chad is telling him the truth or not. He doesn't have time to ask him. The fourth quarter starts. Carolina begins the quarter by getting stuffed three straight times. A short punt gives San Francisco good field position. They are going to keep it on the ground, that's for sure. On the first play, Hearst runs up the middle and coughs up the ball. Carolina falls on it. Gogan pushes a Panther away and rushes over to Chad. His purple face is now blotched with sweat and specks of blood.

"Jesus Christ, Chad, Gilbert's got his hand in my face all fucking day long! Drop a flag, willya? Fuck."

On the next play, Ken Norton drives his helmet into Fred Lane's biceps and Lane fumbles. It's 49er ball right back again. Detmer fades back and hits Rice on a slant. The ball squirts out of his hands, and Eric Davis falls on it. Three plays, three straight fumbles. Hochuli signals Carolina ball! Chad runs over to Hochuli.

"I think his knee was down, Ed. I don't think it was a fumble."

Hochuli looks like the wind's been knocked out of him. His view was blocked on the play, and he didn't have a clean angle of the fumble. If Chad's positive Rice's knee was down, he'll reverse the call. He'll have to. Capers will shit a Buick, but he can't think about that right now.

"If you're sure, I'll reverse it, Chad."

Chad holds up two big former lineman's palms. "I'm not sure. It was close, but I'm not sure."

"Then we have to let it stand."

"Then let's let it stand."

Hochuli rotates his arm in a circle to start the clock.

Beuerlein is sick of this. He drops back on the first play and lays one right into Wesley Walls's lap. Walls one-hands it again and is tripped up on the two yard line. The first man to celebrate is William Floyd, who goes in search of Norton.

"See that, Kenny, you see that? We gonna do it! I'm coming right at you, man, right at you!"

Norton points his finger at Floyd. "You come at me, man. You do that."

He does. Floyd plows into the end zone, carrying Ken

Norton with him. There is deadly silence as none of the officials gives the touchdown signal. Finally, Chad turns to the back judge: "He's in."

"Let me up!" Floyd screams at Norton, who's got his arms wrapped around Floyd's legs. Norton's not letting him go.

Chad taps Norton. "Let him up, Ken."

Norton reluctantly releases Floyd. Floyd prances into the end zone. "Yesss! Yesss! I told you! I told you! We win! We win! We win!"

Kasay's kick is good and Carolina goes back on top, 23–22.

McQuarters runs back the kickoff to the Carolina forty. Flags fly. The run is called back to the twenty. Holding. The crowd goes berserk. The Niners start their final drive. Detmer hits Owens on a slant up the middle. Less than three minutes left. The ball rests on the Carolina forty-seven. Detmer wobbles a pass up the middle that Rice catches. Hearst rambles up the sideline for ten more. He stiff-arms a cornerback. Two-minute warning.

Gogan douses himself with water. "Now, Chad, this is a game."

"You bet, Kevin."

"You want us to win, right, Chad?"

"Yes, I do, Goge. Just as much as I want Carolina to win."

Gogan spits. "You officials are all alike."

Chad manages a smile.

It's true, in a way, all officials are alike. Players, on the other hand, are forged from different molds.

There are your basic multimillion-dollar conglomerate slash pitchmen slash quarterbacks, wide receivers, and running backs, the celebrities and franchise players whom everyone pays to see. Then there are your high-profile hitters, linebackers and defensive backs, the flashy dressers and troubled ones, the club animals, the ones most likely to appear in drug dens, police blotters, or therapy.

Last, but not least, there are the blue-collar workers, the ditchdiggers, field-workers, the nameless, faceless men of steel who toil in the trenches, bloodied but un-bowed.

The men of the meat grinder.

These are our heroes, the men we celebrate.

The two guards and center on offense and the defensive linemen they face off against every Sunday.

While we revere everyone in the grinder (Chad was once a member himself), there are certain players who stand above the rest, those who demand special recognition. They are the all-stars, the ones who not only excel at the mechanics of their positions but also display a gift beyond any of their respected behemoth brethren: the wondrous ability to bitch, moan, and trash-talk at a level of excellence never before seen in the National Football League. In short, with all due respect, the following men have, on occasion, become three-hundred-pound pains in the ass.

Meet the All–Chad Brown All–Meat Grinder Team.

Kevin Gogan, six-seven, 350 pounds

Without question, the MWP of the meat grinder. That's right, MWP—Most Whining Player.

More than any other player in the grinder, Gogan, the winner of *Sports Illustrated*'s coveted "Dirtiest Player in the National Football League," works you. He starts by basking in the recognition of the award, which he knows affords him, at the very least, respect and, at the most, fear. This is a good thing when your business is to engage in hand-to-hand combat every Sunday for six months.

The other way Gogan works you is by talking the talk. He starts the instant he charges through the tunnel for the introduction of the players and goes until the final gun. It's loud incessant talk. Insults, jokes, jibes, jabs, curses, taunts, and whines. Sometimes in the same sentence. The beauty part is that this verbal semisonic assault is directed not just at onrushing defensive linemen but also at the umpires who are trying to police him.

Gogan is no mere crybaby. No one works harder in the grinder. Nobody cares more about beating his man. That's not even enough. Gogan wouldn't feel comfortable just beating him. He wants to crush him, *dominate* him. He *must;* it's his quest. And he will do anything necessary, *anything*, to win. Translated, he needs, as often as possible, to pancake his opponent. He will hold, tackle, chop if necessary, although he viciously denies that, and will do the dozens on you before, during, and after he holds, tackles, or chops. He'll find your weakness and attack it, go right there, go right for it like a shark homing in on a pool of blood.

It was preseason, 1994. The Oakland Raiders, with Kevin Gogan their starter at tackle, were at Seattle playing the Seahawks. It was a typical Gogan game: bumping, bruising, a lot of blood, tons of talk, and a couple of holding calls. After Chad dropped his second flag on him for holding, both in the first quarter, Gogan started directing all of his talk at the umpire.

"I have to be honest with you, Chad. You know I'm a straight shooter, so let me just tell you, right to your face, you are the worst umpire in the league. No, I take that back. You're the worst *official* in the league. How many officials are there in the National Football League? Give me a number."

"I don't know why I'm telling you this, but a hundred thirteen."

"A hundred thirteen? Then I'm guessing they ranked you a hundred *fourteenth*? Am I right? I know I'm right."

"Just play the game, Gogan. It's the first quarter. We got a long way to go."

"Can I ask you something?"

"What?"

"Are you legally blind? Because if you are, then call an official's time-out and go get your Seeing Eye dog. We can wait. Nobody's going anywhere. I mean, that's the only explanation for these holding calls. You can't *see*. That's it, that's gotta be it. You can't be that bad. Nobody can be that bad. You gotta be blind. Remind me never to drive with you."

"Don't worry."

"I just can't believe it, that's all. Those holding calls. I mean, Jesus. Don't you have to take a course or something? Don't you have to be certified or pass some sort of test to become an NFL official? Or do they just give striped shirts and whistles to the first seven guys who show up at the game? By the way, I'm reading a good book. I think you'd like it. I'll get you a copy. I just gotta stop by the Braille Institute on my way home."

And so on. Nonstop through the rest of the first half, all the third quarter, and deep into the fourth quarter.

Late in the game, Oakland put together a crisp four-minute drive to nail down the game, largely behind the punishing blocks of Gogan. As Gogan got into his three-point stance, sweat coursing down his face, his nostrils blasting out streams of air like a bull, Chad studied the lineman's hands. Gogan's fingers rested on the grass, brushing the chalk of the twenty-yard line. The quarterback began shouting his cadence. And then Gogan did it and Chad saw it. Clear as day.

Gogan's right hand moved.

Not much. But just as Gogan got ready to begin his block, his fingers, as they steadied his massive 350-pound frame above him, slightly, almost imperceptibly, *wiggled*.

Chad hurled his flag as if he'd just witnessed Gogan twist off a noseguard's helmet with his head still inside.

Gogan stood, mitts on hips, glaring at Chad. "What the . . . ?"

"What do you got?" asked Markbreit.

"False start, Number 66."

"Really?"   •

"Oh, yeah. Gogan moved his body before the snap of the ball. His whole body was fishtailing all over the place. Can't move your body like that. Gotta work on that fishtail, Goge."

But Gogan's back was to him. His head was down and his shoulders were shaking.

The one thing he didn't want Chad to see was that he was laughing.

Later that week, Chad viewed Gogan's false start in living color on the weekly training tape.

"Now, this is a *K-Mart* call," the voice-over announced.

He's right, Chad admitted. *It was a pretty bad call.*

Suddenly, Chad smiled. He remembered that after the false start, Kevin Gogan, incredibly, stopped whining for the rest of the afternoon.

It might have been a Woolworth call on the tape, thought Chad. *But if it got Gogan to shut up, I make it a Gucci call.*

Gilbert Brown, six-two, ???? pounds

Gilbert Brown has a problem.

As the old joke goes, he has a weight problem. He can't *wait* for his next meal.

At first glance, Gilbert Brown may not seem worthy of a slot in the All–Chad Brown All–Meat Grinder team. Basically, all Gilbert does is clog up the middle. That's not exactly news. It would be news if he couldn't. Granted, he does appear to have limitations. For example, he doesn't play every down. He's been known to skip a whole quarter while he sucks down oxygen and inhales a crate of smelling salts. And he can't really rush the passer. He can't really rush *anything*. He might, on occasion, *waddle* toward the passer, but that's about it. He's not particularly tough and he's not very mean. He doesn't complain about being held. He doesn't gripe about Chad's calls. He doesn't use colorful or controversial language. He's not unusually annoying or particularly difficult.

So why, then, would Gilbert Brown be included as a member of the All–Chad Brown All–Meat Grinder team?

Because no matter what city you're in, Gilbert knows all the best places to eat.

Look at him. It makes sense. And look at the men in the meat grinder. Big slabs of beef, all of them, and every one of them *loves* to eat. Most *live* to eat. Gilbert Brown not only deserves to be a charter member of the team; he's proven to be *invaluable*. One time, and one time only, he needed Chad's help.

Vikings–Packers. 1998. Gilbert huffs over to Chad during a time-out. He looks upset.

"Hey, Chad, I've got to talk to you."

"What's the matter? Randall holding you?"

Chad glances at Randall McDaniel, Minnesota's All-Pro offensive guard but, more important, a future member of the All–Chad Brown All–Meat Grinder Team.

"Nah. Nothing like that."

"Then what is it?"

"Remember last year when we played in San Diego and I went up to LA for dinner?"

"Sure."

"It's killing me, man. I can't remember the name of the restaurant I went to. The one you turned me on to."

"Oh, yeah. What is the name of that place?"

"Come on, you've got to think of it. I have been having such a craving for that chicken."

"I'll get it," Chad says, adjusting his cap. He thinks for a moment, then grins at Gilbert Brown triumphantly. "Aunt Kizzy's."

"That's it! Aunt Kizzy's Back Porch! That's the one! Chad, you have *got* to get me some of that chicken."

"How am I supposed to do that?"

"Send it to me."

"Send you fried chicken from LA? Gilbert, come on, they must have some good down-home fried chicken in Green Bay."

Gilbert stares at him. "Chad, think about what you just said."

"OK, fine. But how the hell am I gonna send you fried chicken from Aunt Kizzy's?"

"Don't they do takeout?"

"Sure they do takeout but . . ."

Gilbert shrugged. "Airfreight me, baby."

Leaving Chad gaping after him, Gilbert Brown wobbles back to his huddle, satisfied, having made his point.

In the meat grinder, you need hard hitters, tough blockers, and strong pass protectors.

You also need somebody who knows food.

Randall McDaniel, six-six, 325 pounds

As Randall McDaniel rumbles back into his huddle, he feels Chad's eyes on him.

"Why do you keep doing that?" McDaniel asks.

"Doing what?"

"Looking at me like that."

"I'm not looking at you."

"Chad," Randall sighs with the patience of a parent dealing with an insubordinate child. "Here is why you're not going to catch me. You're not going to catch me because . . . *I'm not doing anything.*"

He stands toe-to-toe with Chad for a moment to allow his pronouncement to have the proper impact. Then he turns and continues on his trek back to the huddle.

He's good, Chad says to himself. *But today's the day. His downfall. His Day of Reckoning. He's gonna slip up and I'll be there. I'm gonna get him.*

There are few players in the National Football League like Randall McDaniel. He holds, as every offensive lineman does, but he holds in such a clever, camouflaged way that Chad, in seven years in the league, has yet to catch him. In a game against the Packers, Chad almost collared him. Randall pulled tight and close against Gilbert Brown. Chad's fingers encircled his flag . . . but wait a minute? It could be a rip. *Damn. I can't do it. I'm just not sure. When I finally flag Randall I have to be positive because if I'm wrong, I'll never hear the end of it. He'll make my life absolutely miserable. He already does. Not because he complains about my calls. There haven't been any calls. He complains about my monitoring of him, my surveillance of him. Says he's innocent, he never holds.*

I'm gonna get you, Randall.

"*Now* what are you looking at, Chad? You want to catch somebody in the act, watch Gilbert. His hands are up in my face the whole half. He's practically picking my nose. Or what about Reggie White? You know how he gets all those sacks? He uses my damn face mask for a chinning bar!"

Randall bends over and gets into his stance. It is the weirdest stance in the National Football League, perhaps in the history of the league. Randall folds his right fist onto the grass and leaves his left hand dangling in mid-air. He shakes his fingers briefly, violently, as if he's drying his nails. Then, bending his knee so that it's nearly scraping the ground, he stretches his right leg all the way behind him. Finally, he points his right foot straight down. It looks like he's standing on his toes, ballet-style. How can he get any thrust from this stance?

He can and he does. Just ask any defensive lineman who's faced him. Randall McDaniel looks awkward, looks as if you could tip him over with a quick rush to his right side. But he *explodes* out of that stance and he's on you like a bear while you're gaping at him, gawking at his awkward style.

Chad ranks Randall as the smartest lineman in the meat grinder. McDaniel has elevated the act of holding into a science. And as in most sciences, it's often not the answer you get, but the question you ask. The key element is not *how* you hold or *who* you hold; it's *when* you hold. Even more critical is when you *release* your hold—that is, the exact and proper moment when you let go of the guy you're holding.

When Chad works a Minnesota Vikings game and Randall McDaniel is in the grinder, he feels like a cop standing on a street corner in front of a ten-year-old kid (Randall) who's flipping him the bird. Chad turns his back to him. He knows the kid's got his finger up. He whips around. Finger's down. Kid's smiling innocently. Chad turns his back. The bird's up. Chad knows it. He can feel it. He bides his time, starts to go, comes back, then *whoosh!* He's facing the kid. Finger's up on the kid's face, scratching his nose. Chad stares. Makes no move to turn around. Kid gazes off, catches Chad's eye. His eyes say, *What? What are you looking at me for? What did I do?* No matter how many times Chad turns around, no matter how many tricks Chad tries, regardless of how long he stands on that corner, he can't catch the kid flipping him the bird.

Chad Brown and Randall McDaniel have been playing the same game for seven years. It's starting to get old. The frustration's wearing on Chad.

"Randall McDaniel gives me more grief than anyone else in the grinder," Chad proclaims.

"Grief?" says Randall, pretending his feelings are hurt. "*I* give you grief? I'm the cleanest player in the league. You're looking at the wrong side of the line, Chad. You have to look at the defense. Bruce Smith, Reggie White, Warren Sapp, those are the guys you have to watch, those are the culprits. I mean, they're getting away with murder, doing nasty things to me all day long. You would be justified throwing your flag on them on *every* play. But me? I'm going to say it one last time. You don't have to focus on me, you don't even have to look at me because . . . *I don't hold.*"

I'm gonna get you, Randall. One of these days.
I'm gonna get you.

Bob Whitfield, six-five, 310 pounds

It's November 1987 and we're in the vast and dilapidated Los Angeles Memorial Coliseum. In this venue designed for one hundred thousand people, fewer than fifteen thousand loyalists are seriously rocking the place as Banning High School takes on Dorsey for the Los Angeles High School City Championship. As the ball is snapped and the Banning quarterback steps back to pass, the umpire, Chad Brown, glimpses a takedown on the right side of the grinder. It's quick, even subtle, extremely accomplished for a high school kid. *Wham, swack*, and Number 70, the massive All-City tackle, buries the overmatched onrushing defensive end under his heft. It's a classic. He locks one arm around his opponent's waist, grabs his jersey with the other arm, and pulls. Then he falls on him. Uggh.

Textbook holding.

Chad bullets his flag into the turf and waits.

Sure enough, here he comes, right up in my face. The brash, seventeen-year-old, Stanford-bound, National

Football League future first-round draft pick and guaranteed grief machine.

"*What?* What did I do?" the kid pleads.

Oh, he's going to be good. "Holding, my friend," says Chad calmly.

"*Holding?* Are you kidding me? That was a legal block!"

"Yeah. OK."

"This is a championship game. You can't be going ticky-tack on me all day. It's not fair. And you're wrong."

"Well, either you're lying or my eyes are lying, and guess what? My eyes don't lie. I saw it."

"You saw wrong. I think you're penalizing me because I went All-City. It's not my fault. Blame the *Los Angeles Times*. I didn't vote for me."

Chad's heard enough. He turns and heads upfield. He retrieves his flag, stuffs it back into his belt. He turns back and is face-to-face, once again, with the tackle.

"Mr. Umpire, sir, I did not hold. Look at me, look at my size. Why would I hold? I don't need to hold. That was, no offense, just a bad call."

"I'm losing my patience, All-City. If I were you, I'd just walk away."

Frustrated, his plea falling on deaf ears, the tackle throws up his hands and jogs back to his huddle. But he can't stop himself from getting in the last word to his teammates: "That guy's awful."

Meet Bob Whitfield. One of Chad's favorites among the All–Chad Brown All–Meat Grinder Team. Whitfield is destined to become a perennial, the grinder's version of Norm from *Cheers*, the omnipresent guy on the barstool, the guy you can always count on to be there. Because Chad catches Bob Whitfield holding at least once every year and has since high school.

December 13, 1998. Atlanta is playing New Orleans.

Bob Whitfield sits on the field, straddling the twenty-yard line, doing thigh stretches. As he grimaces through the exercises, he keeps one eye open and inspects both sidelines. He's searching for the officials. He wants to see which crew has been assigned to the game. He locates the back judge, then the field judge. He doesn't recognize them. *So far, so good. I don't believe he's on this crew*, Whitfield thinks with relief. *No, he's not. The coast is clear. I'm gonna be all right today.*

A shadow engulfs him. And then he hears that voice. "Hey, Bob."

Whitfield's heart sinks. "Oh, no," he groans.

"How ya doin'?" asks Chad.

"Bad, now that I know you're working the game."

"Come on. I just call 'em as I see 'em."

"That's the problem. You can't see."

"Bob, it's very simple. Don't hold and I won't drop my flag."

"How many times do I have to tell you?" moans Whitfield. "I do not *hold*."

Chad smiles. "Have a good game, Bob."

The game starts and Bob Whitfield is in a foul mood. Maybe he's having a bad week. Maybe it's something he ate. Or maybe it's just Chad. Whatever it is, by half-time Chad has caught him holding twice and Whitfield is pissed. *One more flag*, Whitfield thinks as he heads into the locker room. *He hits me with one more flag and I'm gonna lose it. I don't care. I'm gonna blow my cool right here on national television.*

In the third quarter, Atlanta mounts a drive behind some neat sideline passes from Chris Chandler to Tony Martin and his big tight end, O. J. Santiago. On first and ten from the New Orleans twenty-three, Chandler crosses up the defense and runs a draw play to Jamal Anderson. Anderson bangs up the middle for fifteen yards, but in his wake a flag floats in the air above him and lands right at the feet of Bob Whitfield. Without hesitation, Ed Hochuli, the referee, signals holding and indicates it's on huge Number 70. That's it. Whitfield snaps. He charges into Chad's face.

"You are just picking on me! You are throwing flags left, right, high, low, *everywhere*!"

"Now hold on, Bob," says Chad.

"No, you hold on! I'm not finished! You're gonna hear me out!"

"Well, let me just tell you something—"

"I'm gonna tell *you* something first! You got no right to treat me this way! I've been in this league too long! I've been in the Pro Bowl. I'm not some rookie coming in here who doesn't know the rules! I know the rules! And you *know* I know them. You got it in for me. I don't know why, I really don't, but we've got a problem. What did I do to you? Huh? Something about me you don't like? Is that it? I wanna know because you keep dropping holding flags on me!"

"It wasn't my flag."

"I mean, I'm *pissed*," Whitfield barrels on. "I'm really pissed. And I know I'm probably gonna get a fine or something for being in your face, but why do you keep doing it? Why? Why do you keep calling me for holding?"

"Bob, I said it wasn't me."

Whitfield blinks twice as if he's got something in his eye. "Excuse me?" Whitfield says.

"It wasn't my call," says Chad for the third time. "It was Hochuli. The referee called it on you."

"The referee?"

"Yeah."

"Oh."

Hochuli stands a few feet away. Whitfield peers at him. Hochuli smiles. Whitfield turns back to Chad. "Not your flag?"

Chad shakes his head.

Whifield kicks at the dirt, then puckers his lips for a second before speaking.

"This is embarrassing," he says finally. "We're on national TV, too. Damn. Well. Sorry, Chad. I didn't mean, you know, what I said."

"Don't worry about it."

Whitfield stares at his cleats for a second, then squints into the sun. "Hot out here today, isn't it?"

"Very."

"Kids OK?"

"Fine."

"All right then. I might have been holding, you never know. A hand can slip, grab a jersey, you know how it is."

"Yes, I do."

"Good call," says Whitfield.

Then, to secure his place on the All–Chad Brown All–Meat Grinder Team, right before he tries to find a hiding place in his huddle, he slaps Chad on the backside.

William Roaf, six-seven, 335 pounds, and Dermontti Dawson, six-three, 325 pounds

Let's get something straight. It's not required to be an expert crybaby or All-Pro complainer to make it onto the All–Chad Brown All–Meat Grinder Team. It *helps*, but it's not required. There are a couple of players who have earned their way onto the All–Meat Grinder team despite the fact that they are gentlemen, men who almost never complain or whine. These are men you wouldn't mind bringing home for dinner (if you had a boxcar full of food), men you wouldn't mind introducing to your wife's best friend. Even their names sound cultured and sophisticated: William Roaf and Dermontti Dawson.

Both are exceptional offensive linemen. Of course, that's not a requirement, either. It just so happens to be the truth. The first thing you notice about William Roaf is his gargantuan size. He admits to weighing 355 pounds, but that's a lie. To Chad's trained eye, he's low, way low. Roaf is more like 360 or 370. But fibbing about his weight is not his only claim to fame. He's distinguished by another, more impressive characteristic, putting him in a lofty position high above his peers.

"William Roaf has, by far, the biggest feet in the National Football League," claims Chad. "They're like canoes. I don't know how anyone gets around him. But the main thing I like about him is his attitude."

The contrast with other members of the meat grinder can be startling.

October 18, 1998. New Orleans at Atlanta. Although billed as a mismatch, the game is surprisingly close. New Orleans, in fact, has led for most of the contest, largely because of the play of William Roaf. Roaf has been dominating his side of the line all day, opening wide holes for the running backs, and protecting the Saints' limited quarterback like he's John Elway. Atlanta is throwing everything at Roaf, so far with no success. They've tried double-teams, stunts, delays, and rotating fresh pass rushers, all with various combinations of players. They try defensive linemen Chuck Smith and Lester Archambeau, both separately and together. They send linebacker Cornelius Bennett behind Chuck Smith and Lester Archambeau. They run defensive back Ray Buchanan on a delay behind Cornelius Bennett. Nothing works. Roaf holds his ground, fends off everybody, two, three at a time.

Finally, in the fourth quarter, as Atlanta pulls ahead by what will be the final score, 31–23, Chuck Smith gets an angle on Roaf and blows by him. Roaf reaches out and grabs Smith by the jersey. It's a desperate measure, an act of frustration at having to fight off half the Atlanta defense all afternoon, but he does it, William Roaf *holds*, and Chad Brown catches him.

Chad, professional that he is, never shows favorites, but in this case he can't help but feel for Roaf, who's blocked his butt off all day. It doesn't matter, Chad still drops his flag. He glances up. Willie is walking toward him. Chad can't believe it. William Roaf, coming over to complain? He never complains. He's the nice guy in the grinder, the accommodator, the grinder's gentleman.

"What's up, Willie?" Chad asks.

"Nothing. Just wanted to say, good call. You got me. He had me beat and I grabbed him."

"Funny," says Chad. "I thought you were coming over to complain." Chad gazes at the Falcons' bench, where he spots Bob Whitfield swigging some Gatorade. "Like some people I know."

"Nope. Just came over to say guilty as charged."

Then, clopping forward on his canoes, William Roaf, All-Pro and All–Chad Brown All–Meat Grinder and Mr. Nice Guy, rejoins his teammates in their huddle, ready to block his ass off for the rest of the afternoon.

The other gentleman in the grinder is Dermontti Dawson, the perennial All-Pro center from the Pittsburgh Steelers. Dawson is a marvel to watch. He is such a master at his position that in seven years in the league Chad had never seen him come close to holding. Then, in November of 1997, Chad dropped the bomb on him.

Pittsburgh Steelers against the Buffalo Bills. Right before the end of the first half, Dermontti, turned around on a pass rush, tackles an onrushing Bills' lineman. It's not even questionable. It's so obvious it's shocking. Chad wonders if he's dreaming.

Did I see what I think I just saw? he asks himself. *Dermontti Dawson holding?*

Chad shakes his head and flings his flag into the pile down below.

Markbreit scoots across the field. "What do you have?"

"You're not gonna believe this, but I got 53 on a hold."

"Fifty-three? You got *Dawson?*"

"Yep. The Great One."

"You sure?"

"Positive. First time I ever caught him."

"First time *anyone's* ever caught him," says Markbreit.

As Markbreit steps off the penalty, Chad brushes shoulders with Bruce Smith, legendary defensive end of the Buffalo Bills.

"You finally caught him," Smith says approvingly. "Good for you."

"It was pretty obvious. I never saw him hold before."

"That's because the man's a magician. He's like that guy in Vegas, what's his name? You know who I mean. David Copperfield, that's who. One minute, Dawson's got his hands all over you, pawing you like a puppy. Umpire looks over and *whoosh!* Magic. Hands are gone. Disappeared. How's he do it? I have no idea. But I'm telling you, man, he's the David Copperfield of the National Football League."

"So you're saying he holds, it's just hard to catch him?"

Bruce Smith leans over and whispers as if he's giving Chad the PIN number to his ATM card.

"The man holds *all the time.*"

Chad watches Bruce Smith lumber back to the line of scrimmage and wonders if it's true: Dermontti Dawson holds as much as anyone; he's just so good at it you can't see him. Then Chad remembers Bruce Smith is a *defensive* lineman, talking about an *offensive* lineman.

He knows immediately that Smith is working him, the way any good member of the meat grinder should. During all of this, the only one not saying a word is Dermontti Dawson.

The half ends. Chad heads toward the officials' locker room to fill out his halftime foul report. Bill Cowher, the Steelers' head coach, catches up to him.

"Chad."

"Hey, Bill."

"Amazing. I really can't believe it. You caught Dermontti holding?"

"Yeah, that's what it was."

Cowher shakes his head like a parent defending his son. "He must've done something really bad for you to drop a flag on him."

"Well, yeah, see—" Chad starts to explain.

"No, that's all right, you don't owe me an explanation. If you saw it, he did it. One thing about you, you know what you're doing."

Chad takes the bait for about ten seconds.

Cowher really knows this game, he admits. *Gotta respect him. So when he says I know what I'm doing, he knows what he's talking about. Yeah. He's probably the best coach in the league.*

But then Chad realizes that Cowher is working him the same way Bruce Smith worked him. Compliments get you everywhere in life, even in the National Football League. No harm in sucking up to the officials.

Sorry, guys. It's not gonna work.

Your ten seconds are up.

Frank Winters, six-three, 322 pounds

Frank Winters, center for the Green Bay Packers, is holding on for his life. The noseguard has gone Bull Rush on him and is about to crunch him into the frozen tundra of Lambeau Field and leave him there, packed into the ice for future generations of linemen to see. There's nothing Winters can do except grab onto the enormous noseguard's back and hang on, like a rodeo clown clinging to a bull. Otherwise, the noseguard gets to Brett Favre, the Packers' billion-dollar baby. And when the bad guys get to Brett, you get to go home. As in, released. Waived. Sent bye-bye. What other centers are available? Yes, it's about protecting your quarterback. That is, after all, your job, after you snap the ball, if it's a pass. But don't be naïve. This is not just an act of nobility or an act of loyalty. This is not the Knights of the Round Table. This is the National Football League. To Winters, protecting the quarterback means, frankly, protecting your own ass. And that's what you're gonna do, as long as you're playing, even if you have to hold, right smack in front of the umpire. Half the time these guys never see you anyway. The newer ones, the rookies and second-year officials, are looking in the backfield, trying to track the quarterback's eyes. The older ones, the ones who've been in the league for ten years, are all over fifty and are too blind or too slow, so you can get away with holding all day long.

Winters is falling. He rolls down the noseguard's back as if he's on a water slide at Six Flags. The noseguard is bearing down on Favre, who's looking the other way. *He's going to be blindsided*, thinks Winters.

The Packers' center stretches out and grabs onto the noseguard's shirt. He pulls on it, nearly tearing it off. The noseguard keeps charging. Winters keeps pulling. The cotton jersey in Winter's fist stretches out at least five feet. And then, anchoring himself on the ground, resembling the lead man in a tug-of-war, Winters hauls the noseguard to the turf.

Chad observes the entire penalty with the rapt attention of a young man attending his first striptease. *This really can't be happening*, he says to himself. *I don't believe he's doing this. He's not going to do that. Yes, he is. He did that. And that, too. Man. What balls. He's doing these things* right in front of me!

Flag.

No-brainer. *Hell, Hochuli's got him, too. The side judge has him. The people at home have him. People watching another channel have him.*

Hochuli announces the foul and the number. Chad picks up his flag, passes Winters on his way toward the sideline.

"Pretty easy call, Frank."

"I know."

"You know?"

"Oh, yeah. And if I couldn't pull him down by his jersey, I would've gotten up and tackled him."

"Wait a minute. You see these stripes? It's the umpire you're talking to."

"I recognize you. Doesn't matter," shrugs Winters. "My job is to protect the quarterback. And that's what I'm gonna do, no matter what. Guy gets by me again, I'll pull off his jersey if I have to."

"This is interesting. Most guys tell me they never hold. Never. Never do, never would. Kind of refreshing, your honesty," admits Chad.

"Let me ask you something. Am I the only guy in the league who's ever admitted to you that he holds?"

"On a regular basis?"

"Or ever."

"Let me think about it." Chad takes a moment. "Yep. You're the only one."

"Only guy in the league who *admits* it?"

"You're the one."

"Man, what a dubious distinction."

Dubious, perhaps, but distinct enough to induct Frank Winters into the All–Chad Brown All–Meat Grinder Team, with a bullet.

Reggie White, six-five, 292 pounds

Now that Reggie White has retired, he should, according to Chad, go into politics.

"Oh, it's you," Reggie says as Chad enters the Packers' locker room before their big game against the Minnesota Vikings. "Hey, everybody, look who we got here. Chad Brown in the house! The best umpire in our league!"

Almost in unison, like an oversize chorus line, the Packers' front four lay down their gloves, gauze, and athletic tape and applaud Chad.

"Thank you," says Chad. "That's very nice. Very sincere. You do this for all the umpires, right?"

"No way. Just for you, C.B. You're our friend."

"Please. I don't wanna hear this."

"What? It's the truth."

"You know what, Reggie, you ought to give up football and go into politics."

"Hey, I'm not ready to hang it up yet. I led the league in sacks last year, remember? Besides, politics is too slimy. Lotta lying. Smear tactics. Saying bad things about your opponents . . ."

"So I've heard."

"Hey, man," says Reggie conspiratorially, "keep your eye on those Vikings. All they do is hold. Every one of them. They especially hold *me*."

Then Reggie White takes a step back and peers at Chad as if he's seen him for the first time.

"Listen to me, going on like this. I don't have to tell *you*. I know you got your eye on them. You're not gonna let them break the rules. No way. You know why?"

"I'll bite. Why?"

"Because you're the best."

"Reggie, I'm telling you, seriously, *politics*."

"Yeah, right," laughs Reggie. "Have a good game, Chad."

"You, too, Prez."

*Bruce Smith, six-five, 275 pounds, and Neil Smith,
six-five, 295 pounds*

Bruce Smith and Neil Smith are not related, but they
could be twins.

It's not because they look alike. They don't. It's not
because they have the same last name. Come on, how
many Smiths are there in the world, a billion? It's not
because they're approximately the same size. Actually,
Bruce is taller, Neil is heavier. Or is it the other way
around? Doesn't matter. Not important. It's not even because they're both outstanding defensive linemen in the
National Football League and have been for years.

It's because, in the meat grinder, where they live
every Sunday, they are mirror images of each other.
Their behavior is so similar, it's eerie. And like actual
identical twins, this dual behavior came about instinctively, without so much as a conversation between them.
Miraculously, they employ the same exact methods of
operation, the same tactic, a tactic that has proven as
effective and as reliable as a head slap. With this particular skill, they have learned they can break down any
offensive lineman in the league, even one who out-
weighs them by seventy-five pounds. When they're on
the field, using this strategy, which they have developed
and now perfected through the years, there is absolutely
no way you can tell them apart. The only thing Chad
knows for sure is that the two Mr. Smiths are, in his
mind, the two best defensive linemen in the National
Football League and that they qualify, without question,
as charter members of the All–Chad Brown All–Meat
Grinder team. All because of this special shared skill that
they have elevated to an art form:

The art of whining.

Now that's *whining*, not mere run-of-the mill, everyday complaining.

Not this sort of thing:

"Hey, Chad, did you see that? Sixty-seven? The guard? He was holding me."

What is *that*? You call that whining? That's nothing. That's weak. Chad Brown scoffs at that kind of whining. Don't bring that whining in here, into his meat grinder.

You wanna whine? You better whine by the dozens. Make it strong. Make it loud. Make it fast. And make it funny. Or shut up and play because Chad's not listening to you. He may not even acknowledge you. These guys, Bruce and Neil Smith, they know how to get to you. They know how to whine:

"Hey, Chad," Bruce Smith says, pointing across the line of scrimmage to a burly Miami Dolphins guard whose uniform is two sizes too small. "You see Number 64 on that play? He was holding me so tight, I thought he was gonna propose marriage to me. Shit. He holds me more than my wife."

Or Neil Smith glaring at an Oakland Raiders offensive lineman who's trying, unsuccessfully, to look innocent: "Chad, I don't want to say he's been holding me all day, but I'm wearing his jersey."

Or Bruce: "He's got his hands up in my face so much I can tell you what he had for breakfast, lunch, and dinner."

Neil: "No, Chad, that wasn't a false start. The guard always lines up *behind* me."

Bruce: "When did the National Football League become the World Wrestling Federation? I didn't know we were gonna get held on every play and nobody was gonna drop a flag. I guess they forgot to give me my script."

Neil: "Chad, if 63 puts his fingers inside my face mask one more time, I'm gonna bite his nails for him."

Bruce: "Let me save you a step, Chad. Don't throw your flag. It's a waste of time. Just leave it on the ground . . . because he holds on every play. Oh, and you might want to check his jersey. I don't want to say he's got an illegal substance on it, but he's leaking oil all over the field. He must be down two quarts."

Neil: "Chad, when did they change the rules? When did they say a legal block was tearing off my jersey with one hand and holding onto my face mask with the other? He keeps doing it, I'm gonna press charges. Assault and battery. Gonna call you in as an eyewitness, too. Oh, sorry, never mind. In order to be an eyewitness, you have to be able to *see*."

And on it goes. All day, every down, whining by the dozens. Once, years ago, Chad briefly considered wearing earplugs while he worked a Bruce Smith or Neil Smith game. He abandoned that idea mainly because it was impractical, partially because it was unfair. Oh, well. Everybody is entitled to complain in the meat grinder. Kind of goes with the territory. It's the Smiths' style that distinguishes them and, depending on your mood, amuses or annoys you. *At least I can rest when their team has the ball*, concedes Chad.

Unless, of course, they're playing each other.

Chester McGlockton, six-six, 300 pounds

Some people love their work. Chester McGlockton *lives* to work, which happens to be playing football. The football field is where Chester feels most comfortable, where he feels most at home. He loves his teammates. He loves practicing with them, playing with them, partying with them, praying with them. He loves working out with them, hanging out with them. He loves his locker, his uniform, his number, his per diem, and the all-you-can-eat buffet that awaits him like a challenge every Sunday.

"That's not all I can eat," he says. "I can eat a lot more."

Chester is big and strong and nice. He looks like a

football player until you look into his eyes, which are soft. This is a good guy.

Hell, he even likes the officials. He likes to talk to them, joke with them, comment on and discuss their calls. But McGlockton doesn't do the dozens. He does math.

A couple of years ago. The Oakland Raiders are facing the New York Giants. Chester is lined up against the Giants' right guard. He charges across the neutral zone just before the ball is snapped. Chad slings his flag.

"What?" McGlockton asks, arms spread wide in question. "What was that?"

"False start," Chad informs him.

"Oh, man," says Chester. "That was a two-cent call."

"A two-cent call? What does that mean?"

"I wouldn't give you two cents for it."

"I get it. In other words, *cheap.*"

"Yeah. Worth almost nothing. Two cents."

Later in the game, the Giants' guard hog-ties Chester from behind and drags him down. Chad's right there, on top of the play, and lobs his flag in the air above the linemen.

"Holding," Chad says, giving Markbreit the Giants' player's number. As Markbreit steps off the fifteen yards, Chad looks expectantly at McGlockton.

"A dollar, dollar and a half."

"Dollar and a half. So, are you saying good call?"

"You kiddin'? Dollar and a half's a *great* call."

"OK," says Chad. "I'm just trying to learn the system. It's like learning the new math."

"It's complicated, but I think you can pick it up."

"I don't know. I hope so."

"I'm optimistic," Chester says.

In the fourth quarter, a couple of the Raiders have a slight difference of opinion with two of the Giants. Fingers are pointed, chests are shoved, names are called, fists are thrown, things are said. Flags fly. Among those involved is Chester McGlockton, who claims he was pushed, he was punched, and he never curses. Still, the penalty goes against the Raiders. Chad marches the Raiders back ten yards. Chester walks shoulder-to-shoulder with Chad, in obvious deep and silent protest.

"OK," says Chad. "What was that call?"

Chester shakes his head sadly. "You owe *me* a dollar," he says.

These, then, are the men of the grinder. The first annual All–Chad Brown All–Meat Grinder Team consisting of the previously mentioned players, and a few additions:

OFFENSE

WHINERS

Kevin Gogan. Randall McDaniel. Bob Whitfield.

GENTLEMEN

Dermontti Dawson. William Roaf.

MR. HONESTY

Frank Winters.

GOOD PLAYERS AND GENTLEMEN (They're Still Young)

Jonathan Ogden. Tony Boselli.

DEFENSE

WHINERS

Reggie White. Bruce Smith. Neil Smith.

GENTLEMEN

Gilbert Brown. Cortez Kennedy.

CHEAPER BY THE DOZENS (Class Clown)

Chester McGlockton.

SONNY LISTON AWARD (Most Intimidating Stare in National Football League)

John Randle.

COACH

Bobby "Today Is Sunday Afternoon, You Will Not Be Working in the National Football League by Monday Morning" Ross.

MEAT GRINDER MWP (Most Whining Player)

Kevin Gogan.

Hands down.

Or hands spread out wide in disbelief as he whines, "Who *me?*"

ANNOUNCERS

Joe Theismann. (Never has a good word to say about the officials. And not one official has a good word to say about him.)

Terry Bradshaw (Honorable mention. Doesn't speak well of the officials, but at least Howie Long knocks him on his ass once in a while.)

OWNER

Al Davis.

There is one more person who deserves to be included on Chad's All–Meat Grinder team: Al Davis. The one and only Al Davis, majority owner of the Oakland Raiders. The same Al Davis who has the reputation for being one of the most controversial and intimidating figures in the National Football League, if not in all of sports.

The Los Angeles Memorial Coliseum, 1994. The Los Angeles Raiders are about to take on the Denver Broncos in an important conference game. Chad Brown completes his usual pregame responsibilities. He checks over his cast report, then writes down the last of any possible uniform violations. Satisfied, he crosses the field on his way to the officials' locker room. Suddenly, almost magically, he's met head-on by Al Davis. Mercurial, unpredictable, egomaniacal Al Davis.

"Hi, Chad," Davis says with a smile. "How you doing?"

Is he talking to me? Chad wonders. Chad peeks furtively around the field. *He must be. There's no other Chad around. There's* nobody *around. Huh. Al Davis. The Al Davis is asking me how I'm doing. Weird.*

"Doing fine," replies Chad.

"And how are Deborah, Trent, and Devin?" Davis asks.

"Deborah, Trent, Devin . . . oh, they're fine, just fine, everybody's fine."

"Good. Glad to hear it. Nice talking to you, Chad."

"Yeah. Same here."

And just as magically as he'd appeared, Al Davis vanishes.

Moments later, Chad hooks up with Jerry Markbreit, who's examining the football field as if he's a prospective buyer.

"Hey, Bubba, saw you *schmoozing* with Al Davis."

"Yeah. Me and Al. We're tight."

"I don't know how he does it, but he knows every official's wife and kids by name."

"Really? That's amazing. I can't believe he went to the trouble to do that." Chad stuffs the cast and equipment reports into his back pocket. "I want to find out his wife's and kids' names."

"Why?" asks Markbreit.

"Because next time I see Al Davis, I'm gonna run the same game on him." Chad grins.

Al Davis and NFL officials? Mortal enemies?

If so, in the words of the late Israeli military genius Moshe Dayan: "Keep your friends close and your enemies closer."

Welcome to the meat grinder, Al.

15
FLAG ON THE PLAY

On fourth down, with thirty seconds left in the game, Wade Richey, the rookie 49ers kicker with the booming but inconsistent leg, tries a forty-six-yard field goal. Carolina tries to ice him with a time-out, but the kid's not rattled. The ball clears the uprights and the 49ers take the lead, 25–23.

During the television time-out, the officials huddle at midfield.

"Down to this," Chad says.

Like the players, the officials have a two-minute drill. Chad's job is to always have a ball in play. After each down, he races at full speed to spot the ball, making sure the offense never loses any time.

Richey prepares for the kickoff. On orders from Mariucci, he boots a low line drive. Mark Carrier catches it at midfield.

In disbelief, Chad hears himself say, "That was dumb."

Carolina has the ball at midfield with twenty-seven seconds left. Kasay has already hit one from fifty-two yards away. Ten yards closer and they can win this game.

Beuerlein fades back to pass.

And then, no doubt about it, Chad Brown sees the Carolina guard reach out and trip Chris Doleman. Nobody else sees it. Hell, Doleman gets up without a word.

A thin smile, an ironic smile, crosses Chad's lips. Because Chad knows that who wins this game will be determined by the call or noncall he's about to make. It's a powerful and complicated feeling. Destiny is wrapped up in the little yellow handkerchief stuffed into his belt.

Chad reaches into his belt and flings the yellow flag.

Hochuli rushes over. "What do we got?"

"Sixty-four. Holding."

Hochuli glances at the sidelines. Dom Capers is motionless. This is a dagger to the heart. Hochuli has no choice. He announces the penalty. Then, stabbing the Panthers in the chest, he moves Carolina back, out of field goal range.

Twenty-four seconds left now. Beuerlein hits Carrier at the left sideline.

Nineteen seconds left. Beuerlein back. He passes. It's dropped.

Eleven seconds left. Beuerlein looks. Norton breaks through the line. Beuerlein scrambles and dumps off a five-yarder to Rocket Ismail.

Four seconds left. Kasay comes onto the field to try a fifty-eight-yard field goal to win the game. The crowd is beyond insane; they're *irrational*. This is not unusual. After all, this is a football game.

Chad steps back into position for the kick. He settles himself by taking a deep gulp of air. You also can't know the smell of football on television. The smell of sweat and tension and victory and loss.

The snap from center is down. The kick is up. Straight and true.

But . . . is it long enough?

The ball hits the crossbar with a clunk and falls back onto the field. Six inches short. San Francisco wins, 25–23.

Gogan pulls off his helmet and races past Chad. "Nice

game, brother. Hey, Chad, when you gonna retire? You're eligible for Social Security, right?"

"Gonna make the Super Bowl first."

"Yeah. Well, see you there."

He's gone.

Then a phalanx of security guards fold themselves around the officials and whisk them off the field.

Behind him, Chad sees William Floyd and Ken Norton hugging.

In the locker room, Chad sits quietly in the corner by the minifridge as Norm Schachter, former NFL referee and this week's observer, goes over the fouls called in the game. Chad has written his fouls down with explanations, in triplicate, on his game report sheet. As Schachter confers with Don Carey, the back judge, and George Hayward, the head linesman, Chad rests a weary forearm on top of the fridge. He slowly rubs his skin, scarred, cracked, and tough as old leather. Suddenly he begins to reflect about the game, the season, and seasons past.

A life in the meat grinder.

A life like any other. The present tense melding with past moments of hysterical laughter, severe disappointment, and aching loss.

A life of irony. Layers of irony. Chad Brown, a quiet, private man, finds himself thrust weekly into a blinding public spotlight, doing his business in front of potentially unruly masses whose opinion of him can vary from, at best, grudging approval to rabid visceral hatred in any given thirty seconds from snap to tackle.

Another irony is the featured role Chad plays in this larger-than-life, out-of-proportion weekly three-hour spectacle when the rest of the week his life resonates with familiarity. By choice, it borders on the mundane. Monday through Friday, Chad is a regular guy with a comfortable job at UCLA. Decent pay, good benefits, cordial coworkers. No spotlight in sight. If he ever found one's beam searching for him, he'd grab it and aim it in the opposite direction.

Life in the meat grinder puts him in the middle of the action. It fits him like a pair of old sneakers. Comfortably. He embraces this life. It is him. It defines who he is, a man who thrives on routine, rigor, and structure. Rules. Chad needs rules. He played by them and now he enforces them. He has come full circle. Nothing will force him to break that circle. He will stay right here in the middle until he achieves the final goal he's set: to be one of the Magnificent Seven, the seven officials who, every January, preside over the single most important annual sporting, entertainment, and commercial event in our land and in our living rooms.

When that goal is met, Chad will happily continue in the Life for a few years more. Then he will probably conduct his own version of a farewell tour. Like a triumphant athlete or performer, he'll travel from city to city and visit the sites of previous glories. Maybe he'll receive some modest acknowledgment or reward. Maybe the younger officials will anoint him, treat him like a prophet or at least a respected elder of his trade, and ask him for tips, secrets, tricks, and, perhaps, wisdom.

Maybe. Doubtful.

After all, he's just a referee.

But right now, in this closet at Three Com, he's got to go over all of his fouls.

Norm Schachter snaps the game report with his forefinger. "Interesting game," he says to Hochuli. Then Schachter turns to Chad. "Tough call there at the end, Chad."

"I know. It stopped Carolina's drive. Might've cost them the game."

"It was the right call. Tough call. But the right call."

For Chad Brown, that is what this life, this life inside the meat grinder, is all about.

OVERTIME
VII

16
THE ROUND TABLE

Friday night, April 30, 1999.

I'm sitting in my hotel room, Room 912 at the DoubleTree, with a couple of friends and one living legend. The hotel's in Westwood, just a few minutes away from my office at UCLA. It's about seven-thirty.

We've just come from the practice field, and we're all pretty tired. We've just put in a whole afternoon on the football field under a hot LA sun. For the last five years I've been running a camp for aspiring football officials. I try to teach them some skills, some mechanics. These are guys, and some women, who are maybe at high school level at best. Most are at Pop Warner. I give them the opportunity to do classroom work with about eight or nine NFL officials, then get on the practice field and work a scrimmage with the UCLA football team, thanks to head coach Bob Toledo. I call my camp the Personal Touch.

But tonight my friends and I feel like rapping. The old-fashioned way, which just means talking. We want to talk about ourselves. We want to talk about what it's like being an official in the National Football League. The truth. These guys know. They are on the field, or have been, every Sunday, for a lot of years. In my opinion, these are some of the best in the business.

They are Chuck Stewart, NFL line judge; Ed Hochuli, NFL referee and my crew chief; and Red Cashion, for-

mer NFL referee, who's nothing less than a living leg-end. Hochuli and Cashion are sitting on the sofa. Chuck is lying across my bed. The tape recorder is running.

CHAD: Give me your names, your positions, how long you've been in the National Football League, and what you do in civilian life.

HOCHULI: Ed Hochuli. Spelled E-d. [Laughter.] I'm a referee in the league. I'm about to start my ninth year. My part-time job is as a lawyer.

CASHION: My name is Red Cashion. I joined the NFL in 1972. I retired in 1996. Most of the time I was a referee. I'm in the insurance business.

STEWART: Charles Stewart. I've been in the National Football League for seven years. I'm a line judge and I'm an administrator for social services programs in my part-time job.

CHAD: OK. Let me start with this question. If you guys were at a party and you didn't know anybody and some-one asked you, "What do you do?" Would you say, "I'm an NFL referee," or would you say, "I'm a lawyer"?

HOCHULI: It depends. There are some parties where I would say I'm a lawyer. For example, if it was a party consisting of business contacts, from the lawyer world. If I were just at a party of friends, just a general party, I'd say I was an NFL referee.

CASHION: Same thing. I think the crowd and location dictate what you say. I think the place you get asked that most often is on an airplane. It hasn't happened to me since last night. [Laughter.] Young lady said to me,

"What do you do?" I said, "Basically, I'm retired. But I used to officiate football." If I were in my local town, at a party, I'd say I was in the insurance business. Nearly anyplace else, I say I'm retired from the National Football League.

HOCHULI: But, Red, I would also think it would be pretty tough for you to go to a party and have people not know who you are. I mean, I'm just a pimple on your butt in terms of people knowing who I am, but it's pretty unusual for me to go into a setting like that and not have at least somebody know who I am. The word spreads.

CASHION: That's true. I live in a somewhat small community, College Station, Texas, so I generally say I'm in the insurance business.

STEWART: I think Red is being a little modest now. Whenever anyone knows I work in the National Football League and they hear that I once worked with Red, that's the first thing everyone wants to talk about: Red Cashion. There is a distinction about him that I don't think anyone else has ever had. Everyone recognizes his first down call. No one has had that kind of personality that's been brought into the league. As far as the question goes for me, when I mention I'm an administrator for social services, everyone always has a cousin who has a need, or they know somebody else . . . [Laughter.] I try to get away from that. Especially if my wife's with me. Quite honestly, she is very proud of the fact that I am in the National Football League. She will bring the topic up.

CHAD: For me, it depends. If I'm in my own town, everybody knows me. I wouldn't need to bring it up. If I'm somewhere else, people will usually start conversations with me because they think I'm—

HOCHULI: Gene Upshaw. [Laughter.]

CHAD: Right. Or some other athlete. The subject comes up, I tell them. But I don't bring up that I'm a referee. I usually say I'm in recreation. I don't like it when people ask me a whole lot of questions about it.

STEWART: I suppose if it's during the season and there's been a lot of controversy, then you might say, "I sell insurance."

CASHION: I don't think so. I prefer the controversy, to tell you the truth. Because that's when I want to take up the side of the officials. I don't sidestep it.

CHAD: I think we've found out this year that one of the things that would help is to talk about the stuff that happens. As opposed to not talking about it.

CASHION: Amen.

CHAD: Some people might say, "Well, they might not want to talk about this. They might not want to talk about a controversial call."

HOCHULI: That sure doesn't stop people from asking.

CASHION: I am very sensitive as to how they ask the question. If they're really interested, or they want to talk about football, I'll talk with them all night. But if they want to talk about how you sorry so-and-sos could miss something that obvious, I don't have any time for them.

CHAD: What is the biggest misconception that the public has about NFL officials?

HOCHULI: That we're part-time.

CHAD: Talk about that.

HOCHULI: During the season, I spend forty hours a week on officiating. At least.

STEWART: More than that.

HOCHULI: People don't have any conception of how much time goes into it. They have absolutely no idea how important it is to all of us and how we *bleed* over any mistake we make. We agonize over it. People just ... they just don't know how important it is.

STEWART: I'd like to echo that.

CHAD: I would, too.

CASHION: This is kind of dangerous because I've been out of it for a couple of years and so it would be pretty easy to say, "Well, you're just trying to hang on." That's really not the case. The thing I truly believe, even more so after being away from it, is that there's an importance, significance, a *feeling*. I used to call it fun. But I think there's a whole lot more to it than that. I think the people who put on these striped shirts are so involved in this game, and it is so meaningful to them, it is not a job. It's more like an art. It means so much to them. Not only to be right but to be able to handle a game, to control a game, make it go like it's supposed to go. Be in the right spot. Do the right thing. Say the right thing. It almost becomes a *passion*. That's why I think these guys are the best officials in the world.

STEWART: I don't know if even the players approach it with the same kind of passion.

CASHION: I've never been a player, so I don't know how they approach it. The difference is, the money is not a factor with these guys.

CHAD: Red's right. We do it for the love of the game.

CASHION: There is a pride that is very, very difficult to describe, and I haven't found it in any other place in sports.

STEWART: When I get something in the mail that says "NFL," that is the first thing I open up. Way before the American Express bill or the phone bill. [Laughter.] As Ed said, there is a misconception about our being part-time. Maybe, technically, we are not full-time officials. But there is not a football game that is played that we don't officiate. And we are held to a higher standard than other people are in the league. That can be good and bad. But when I get off an airplane coming home after a ball game, I can never go to sleep. We have a satellite dish. My wife tapes every game that I do. There are invariably four or five plays I'm gonna go and watch. Coming from the East Coast to the West Coast, I may get in at eleven-thirty or twelve. By the time I get home it's one o'clock. I am going to watch those four or five plays, sometimes an entire half of the game, before I go to bed that night. When Monday night comes along, I look at that game and the second half of my ball game. Some people may think I'm crazy. I don't care. I take a lot of pride in what I do. I want to be the best I possibly can.

CHAD: People will accept imperfection in players; you've seen that. Why does the public feel that the officials have to be perfect?

STEWART: You have the same thing in society. People don't accept law enforcement officers when they step beyond the boundaries, or happen to make mistakes. We are the police on the football field.

CHAD: Let me read you something and get your reactions. Ray Bentley, a FOX-TV broadcaster, said, and, I want to warn you guys, this is pretty inflammatory [reads]: ". . . that was the worst officiating I've ever seen. There were so many non-calls. The league has to do something. It's about time they stopped having old men trying to chase around the best athletes on the planet." What do you think?

HOCHULI: The guy who worked the Super Bowl last year at back judge was sixty-five years old. Retired at the end of the season. Don Hakes. Retired as the number-one back judge in the league. Don Hakes was on an entirely different plane than the rest of the back judges, he was so good. And he was sixty-five years old. Officiating is an occupation that you only get good at with a tremendous amount of experience. You don't need to be fast. You need to have judgment. You need to understand where the play's going, so you're in the right place to make the call. I remember when I used to play racquetball a lot. I'd play with some old-timers. They'd never move and they'd have me running all over the court. They'd always know where the ball was going to go when I'd hit it. That's kind of the way football is.

CHAD: Sometimes it's not where you are or how fast you get there; it's what you see. It's your vision. This guy doesn't talk about knowing the game or what to look for.

STEWART: It's so interesting because he was able to make those observations sitting in the press box or at home, watching his television set. We are always ten feet to fifteen yards away from the play. We are also looking at a different thing than what he's looking at. We are trained to watch certain things, sets, certain people on the field. The average fan is going to follow the football. Television is going to follow the football. The announcers are going to follow the football. We are not going to watch the football. We are going to watch our keys in our area.

CASHION: I also believe that the number-one ingredient of an official at this level is an item called presence. I have seen very, very few young people who have presence.

CHAD: Can you describe what that is? What is presence?

CASHION: Presence is walking into a classroom with a 240-pound assistant coach. He's screaming at the kids, telling them to shut up, and it just gets louder. You walk into the next room and there's a fifty-six-year-old grandmother in there about five-feet-two. She says, "Class." And *whoom*. Quiet. That's presence.

CHAD: And there are some officials who have it?

CASHION: There are a lot of officials who have it.

CHAD: I want to say something here. I think what Red was saying is that when you're young, you don't have presence. Sometimes it takes a little maturing. I think Ed hit it right on the head. You can take a young guy who's an athlete and he can come into certain situations and play right away. But if you're a young official, it's going to take you some time. It's experience that makes you good. It's tough to officiate that ball game. It took me, really, seven years to learn how to feel comfortable being an umpire. I knew what the game was all about. I knew what a block was. A low block. Where you could block, when you could chop in the line of scrimmage. I didn't quite understand what holding was. I knew what it was supposed to be, but I had to find out what the company I worked for wanted. Same thing at UCLA. You have to learn the ropes. Your skills may diminish a little bit as you get older. But I don't think that has anything to do with what call you make. The older you get, the better you get. Donnie Hakes? I bet he can still referee another three, four years.

HOCHULI: No question. You know, you asked about misconceptions before. . . . A very significant misconception that I just drew a blank on . . . people really don't understand how good the officiating is in the NFL. People are not aware that there is a grading system. The league office spends six to eight hours grading, in slow motion, in stop action, in back and forth, every official, on every play. They've got, not just the TV package, but they've got three other angles on the game. Three other tapes. They go through it all. If we made a tenth as many mistakes as the announcers suggested we make, we'd be fired. Officials get fired every year because their grades aren't up to standard. Those grades determine who works play-offs, who works the Super Bowl. We are under a tremendous amount of scrutiny by people who really understand the game. The announcers . . . this is an entertainment industry . . . no different than the movies or TV or anything. The announcers make it *entertaining*. A lot of times controversy is what's entertaining. How do talk show hosts get calls? By saying controversial things. They might not even believe it. But it gets people to call.

CHAD: Funny, huh? At our age, we still get report cards.

HOCHULI: How many people work a job where their boss videotapes their work from every different angle and then analyzes it in slow motion?

CHAD: There is not another job in the world that is scrutinized the way officials are.

HOCHULI: Including other sports officials. For some reason, football officiating is held to a higher standard than any other sport. I was watching a baseball game the other day. The announcers commented on how the umpire was wrong on a call at second base. They said, "That's the same guy who missed that one in the first inning." That was it. They just went on, didn't say anything more. If we missed two calls in the same game like that? They'd be all over us!

STEWART: Another misconception. Most people believe that I get on an airplane, fly to a city that morning, do the ball game, and go home. They have no idea of what it takes to even . . . The game itself is the easiest thing I do during the week!

CHAD: It is, by far.

STEWART: The *preparation* is the most difficult.

CASHION: Also, after a game, after you take a shower, you are tired. I don't mean physically tired. I mean mentally tired.

HOCHULI: Oh, it's an emotional drain.

CASHION: It's just a high. You build yourself up so high.

CHAD: Can anyone put a finger on what causes you to be at such an emotional peak?

CASHION: I think it's because it's such an effort in concentration. That's what builds it up. Officiating is an exercise in concentration. I think anything that you concentrate on that hard, that long, takes you to an emotional high that is very difficult to come off of.

CHAD: This leads me into instant replay. Is this a good thing? It didn't work before. Why will it work now? Is this going to help us do a better job?

STEWART: I've given a lot of thought to instant replay. It is not going to change how I do a ball game, whatsoever. If instant replay happens to see where I made a mistake and we can correct it right then and there, I'm more than happy to have it. I think you're going to see that we are right most of the time.

HOCHULI: If replay can fix a mistake that I made, wonderful. All of us want to be right. I think replay can be successful if people will accept, and I don't think they can, that replay can't make it perfect. That's why I think instant replay is doomed. If people will accept that replay will fix some of the big mistakes, but that's as good as it can do, then I think replay can be a valuable tool. The downside to replay is that, well, let me tell you a very quick story. The very first Monday night game I worked was in Chicago. The Jets and the Bears. It went into overtime. Thirteen seconds left in the game. Jim Harbaugh completed a pass to their tight end, Cap Rocco. I remember this like it was yesterday. He gets tackled on the goal line. I'm the back judge. I'm the one standing there, doing this. [Gives touchdown signal.] Six points. The teams were in the locker room and they reversed it. We had to go into the locker room and bring the teams back out. The quarterback runs a quarterback sneak, scores a touchdown. The lowest moment in my officiating life. My stomach knots right now when I think about it. I go into the office the next day and my partners are giving me the touchdown signal in the hall. I got stick figures on my desk giving touchdown signals. Wednesday of that week the league office calls. They say, "We got the other replay from NFL films over your shoulder. You were correct. It was a touchdown." [Pause.] Replay doesn't have the same *angle*. There are too many times that we have all seen when the next films come in, they come in on Tuesday, there are lots of other film besides TV, and they show a different angle, and they show a different result. Sometimes, with replay, the view you see on TV is wrong. So, sometimes, what we will do, because of replay, is the wrong thing to do. It's good that the officials are making the decision on the field because then we are able to combine what we saw in three dimensions with what's on the screen in two dimensions.

CHAD: In the old system, almost a fourth of the reversals were wrong.

HOCHULI: Yep.

CASHION: I think the fans have demanded replay. I personally think replay will be good for the officials. It will add a tremendous amount of credibility. I think the system itself, when you get right down to it, is quite a tribute to the officials because in their wisdom in putting it together, other than the last two minutes, they say, basically, we can't make but two mistakes. I mean, what a compliment. They say there are only going to be two errors in the game. The problem I have with instant replay is that you talk about using it, but nobody really talks about what it's supposed to do. If it's supposed to prevent an error, then why limit it to two? Does that mean we are only going to correct two errors? I'm going to predict that instant replay will be used until it gets expanded, like it did before, to the point of interruption. Then it'll get shut down again.

CHAD: It'll be abused.

CASHION: It'll be abused. Because you don't know exactly where to stop it. I'll give you an example. Right now the rule says if you go to the sideline and you fumble at the sideline, you can use instant replay to determine who recovers the ball. You have a play where you get a receiver, and I'm asking you all this, who gets hit three yards in bounds, and as he gets hit the ball comes out and now rolls out-of-bounds. As I understand it, you can use instant replay for that.

CHAD: Yeah.

CASHION: Well, suppose he gets hit right smack in the middle of the field. They say we're not going to use it in the middle of the field. But say he gets hit so hard that the ball comes loose and it rolls all the way out-of-bounds. Now can we use instant replay?

HOCHULI: I think so. We haven't been given all the guidelines at this point. We don't know all the things it's going to cover. Right now it's pretty broad as to the things that can be covered.

CHAD: Just about everything.

HOCHULI: I think replay, frankly, is going to be used very little except in the last two minutes of the two halves. I don't think coaches are going to use their time-outs on it unless it's a huge play. The real stoppages will come in the last two minutes of each half. Those are going to be a real problem because that's giving a team an advantage. When you stop a game to look at instant replay, suddenly that team gets a time-out without having to use one. That's going to have a significant effect on the two-minute drive.

CHAD: In other words, using instant replay can change the momentum.

HOCHULI: Yes.

CASHION: Here's a play. San Francisco's got the ball, driving in. The ball's on the five-yard line. With nine seconds left to play, they dive for the goal line. The official says he doesn't make it. When they blow the whistle to stop the play, there are four seconds left on the clock. Now the guy upstairs is not quite sure. Does he shut it down?

HOCHULI: If he does, they get another shot.

CHAD: If they line up, with four seconds left, they're going to get that play off.

HOCHULI: See, that's the thing. Instant replay isn't going to stop controversy. It's going to change what the controversy is. Should we have reversed it? Should we have stopped it? Those kinds of things. There's going to be just as much controversy.

CHAD: I actually think instant replay is going to go away. I think it's going to blow up in their faces. I really do. I think they are going to expand it and expand it and then it's finally going to go away. Forever.

STEWART: With instant replay, aren't they questioning the job we do?

CASHION: If the owners want instant replay, the officials have no reservation about using it. It's their game. We'll call whatever they want. They make the rules. If the rules include instant replay, these guys will include that as part of the game. The question is how much will it change the game? The one thing I am absolutely positive of, if you let the officials stand on their record, they will come out on top.

CHAD: Are there any other changes, any other rules, you would like to see instituted?

HOCHULI: My answer to that one is I don't care. I'll officiate the rules the way they put them in. I think the competition committee over the years has done a marvelous job of making football a very entertaining game. When you look at the TV ratings for any old average Monday night game and it blows away the seventh game of the World Series, or game seven of the NBA championship, it tells you they've done something right with football.

CHAD: Why is this the best job in the world? Or why would some people see it as the worst job in the world? And would you want your kids to become NFL officials? Now let me answer my own question first. [Laughter.] I think it's the best job for me because it keeps me in touch with the game that I love. I've been playing this game ever since I was a kid. When I could start walking. I'm a very competitive individual. Officiating kind of puts you in a situation where you are using some of the same instincts and skills that you used as a player. Except you're using them to keep the game honest. I like both sides of it. I may have liked the other side a little bit better. I liked the contact. I enjoyed taking on another guy one-on-one. I got a charge out of that. This is still competitive. I would do it without the money. I thrive on the challenge that's involved. As far as my kids go, I think they will become officials. At least one of them, I'm pretty sure, will become involved in it. They like it. They want to come into the hotel, hang out with the guys. The only part about the job I don't like is the negativity. I don't know if I'd want my kids to be scrutinized from a negative standpoint all the time. It's a business in which they're always looking for mistakes.

HOCHULI: It's like an upset stomach. You don't even know you've got a stomach unless it's upset. [Laughter.] They don't talk about the good stuff. They only talk about the bad stuff. That's the way the public is.

STEWART: Those individuals who are National Football League officials, these are the elite. You are the best. It is great to be in this fraternity. My best friends are National Football League officials. But to be in this fraternity, you have to have talent.

CHAD: I think you need talent. But I think the most important thing you need is good instincts. Officiating to me, well, it's not the same talent you look for in a great running back or a good guard. It's concentration.

CASHION: First of all, I wasn't good enough to play football. But I loved it. Officiating enabled me to be involved with it. But that's not quite as important to me as the second point, which I think is rather unique. That unique part is right here. I take this guy right here [puts hand on Hochuli's shoulder] . . . and I compete against him as an official as hard as I know how to compete. I mean, I put everything I have into being better than he is. But I absolutely love him.

CHAD: I feel the same way, too. I feel the same way about guys in my position, like Ron Botchan. He's been talked about as the best. The biggest thing for me to do is knock him off that throne. But I like that guy, I really do. I just want to be the best. It brings back the competitiveness. It's like when I was in college, I wanted to be an All-American. I worked my ass off to get it. I want to be the best in everything I do. Hell, I want to be the best recreation guy! I want to be the best umpire. And I'm gonna get it.

CASHION: But I bet you don't feel toward the guys in recreation the way you do about the three guys in this room.

CHAD: No. I don't. You're right. You're absolutely correct.

CASHION: I love all three of these guys. I mean that. I'm using the word. I'll flat tell you, I love you guys.

HOCHULI: There is incredible camaraderie among all 113 officials. Incredible. I often watch a golf tournament, for example, and it's coming down to the eighteenth hole, the last round, and I'm wondering, *Is he hoping that guy misses the putt?* Probably so. I don't think Chad is hoping that Ron Botchan makes a mistake. Chad is pulling for Ron Botchan *not* to make a mistake. His competition with Botchan is that he's going to do even better. The reason this is the best job in the world for me is, first of all, I love the game. I think that's a requirement. I, too, am extremely competitive. But I really don't ever feel that I'm competing with the other referees. I'm competing with myself. I have never seen another avocation or occupation where anyone is put to the test anywhere near the way I am with officiating. I am a trial lawyer by trade. I don't have anywhere near the stress in the courtroom that I do on the football field. I am in front of literally a hundred million people who are going to watch what I do in slow motion and stop action. I've got to make a decision just like that. I'm going to be right or wrong. Everything else is subjective. This isn't. I'm either right or wrong. That competition to myself, to get it right, and the satisfaction, under all of those circumstances, and that pressure, the pressure of being right, is just a *rush* in a way that I can't explain.

CHAD: Amen. And I think that's a good place to stop. Thank you.

CASHION: I just want to say, probably the most difficult position on the field is the umpire position. With all the things you have to do. Your ability, Chad, your ability to be in that role, and control those people in the middle, and to have the stature, not only because of your size, but because of the way you work . . . [looks at others in the room] . . . this guy will end up being one of the real great umpires in the National Football League.

CHAD: That's nice, Red, thank you. I hope I do end up being a great umpire in this league.

CASHION: You will. Hell. I guarantee it.

POSTGAME
VIII

It's a surreal scene.

Two chartered buses pull into the circular driveway of the DoubleTree Inn in Westwood, a few minutes from UCLA. The doors to the buses hiss open, and a stream of football referees, all in full uniform, pile out. One can tell immediately by the plastic shopping bags in their hands and the hesitant looks on their faces that these are not NFL officials.

They are students, in a way, students of football. They are in Los Angeles to learn the art of officiating at Chad Brown's Personal Touch Football Camp. Each one has shelled out $300 for the three-day instructional clinic. A quick check of the roster reveals eighty-three participants, including three women. There is someone from nearly every state, and one referee has flown in for the weekend from Tokyo. All this to spend a few hours listening to training tips and war stories from the National Football League's finest, among them Chad Brown, Ed Hochuli, Red Cashion, Chuck Stewart, and Johnny Grier. Whatever Chad is doing, though, it must be working. Many of the campers are repeaters, some for the third or fourth time. A few have become devotees. This year, in a heated live auction battle, a referee's shirt signed by Jerry Markbreit went for almost seven hundred dollars.

Saturday morning, on the way to a campus practice field where the campers will have an opportunity to work some reps with the UCLA football team, Chad weaves his forest green Jeep Cherokee through Westwood traffic. Ed Hochuli occupies the backseat. Chad drives in silence. Something is troubling him. He holds at a red light, leans his head back to Hochuli.

"Did you know that out of the eighty campers, there are twenty-five umpires? Damn. That is a lot."

"That is a lot," agrees Hochuli.

"Why do you think there are so many umpires?"

"Why?"

It's a rhetorical question to Hochuli. The answer is obvious. But not to Chad. Hochuli waits for Chad to see it. To do that, Chad would have to put himself in the spotlight. He truly, genuinely, cannot do that. Chad was born minus the hoopla gene. Hochuli, aware of this but often surprised by it, decides to take it upon himself to enlighten him.

"They came because of you, Chad."

For a moment Chad says nothing. He is too modest to accept this.

"You think so?"

Hochuli only smiles. "You're the draw, big guy. The star attraction."

Chad seesaws his head slightly. *Maybe. Maybe there is some truth to that. It's hard to accept, though. Hard to believe that I have achieved this level of success. I sure never saw it coming. Sneaked up on me like a mugger. A draw. The reason people came here. To see me. I'm not sure I'm ready for this.*

He gives it one more try, one more dis.

"Naw. I don't think so. They're not coming for me."

"Tell you what," suggests Ed Hochuli. "Offer the same camp next year, only say in the brochure that you won't be here. Then tell me how many umpires show up."

"Hmm."

Chad turns to the window, glances at a couple of students slouching into Starbucks.

Then, for some odd reason, he thinks of Sam Huff.

Did he know? Did Huff know when he made it? When he reached his goal, his goal to be the best at his position in the National Football League, the best ever?

I'm not there. I'll be there when I get to the Super Bowl. When I'm the first black umpire to work that game. I've still got a ways to go. Still got a lot of work vto do. A lot of tapes to watch, tests to take, guys to police in the meat grinder. Long way to go.

No. I'm not there.

Not yet.

But I am gonna get there.

I know I am.

In the words of Red Cashion, "I guarantee it."

MORE WINNING SPORTS BOOKS
FROM ST. MARTIN'S PAPERBACKS

MARCUS:
The Autobiography of Marcus Allen,
with Carlton Stowers
From his triumphant rise to football stardom to his friendship with O.J. Simpson, get the real story—in his own words—on Heisman Trophy winner Marcus Allen.

HANG TIME:
Days and Dreams with Michael Jordan,
by Bob Greene
Journalist and bestselling author Bob Greene follows sports legend Michael Jordan for two seasons with the Chicago Bulls, and uncovers some amazing things about the athlete—and the man.

MICHAEL JORDAN, by Mitchell Krugel
A head-to-toe portrait of basketball's phenomenal Michael Jordan—on and off the court, in intimate detail.

THIS GAME'S THE BEST!
So Why Don't They Quit Screwing With It?
by George Karl with Don Yaeger
The fiery, funny, outspoken head coach of the Seattle Supersonics cuts loose on the sport of basketball and all its players.

AVAILABLE WHEREVER BOOKS ARE SOLD
FROM ST. MARTIN'S PAPERBACKS